Are You Happy

M.L.Ruscsak

Are You Happy

Copyright © 2021 by Trient Press

All rights reserved. No part of this publication may be reproduced, distributed, or transmitted in any form or by any means, including photocopying, recording, or other electronic or mechanical methods, without the prior written permission of the publisher, except in the case of brief quotations embodied in critical reviews and certain other noncommercial uses permitted by copyright law. For permission requests, write to the publisher, addressed "Attention: Permissions Coordinator," at the address below.

Criminal copyright infringement, including infringement without monetary gain, is investigated by the FBI and is punishable by up to five years in federal prison and a fine of $250,000.

Except for the original story material written by the author, all songs, song titles, and lyrics mentioned in the novel The Silent Wars are the exclusive property of the respective artists, songwriters, and copyright holders

Trient Press
3375 S Rainbow Blvd
#81710, SMB 13135
Las Vegas,NV 89180

Ordering Information:
Quantity sales. Special discounts are available on quantity purchases by corporations, associations, and others. For details, contact the publisher at the address above.
Orders by U.S. trade bookstores and wholesalers. Please contact Trient Press: Tel: (775) 996-3844; or visit www.trientpress.com.

Printed in the United States of America

Publisher's Cataloging-in-Publication data
Ruscsak, M.L,
A title of a book : Are You Happy
ISBN Hardcover : 978-1-955198-21-9
    Paperback : 978-1-955198-22-6
    E-book :   978-1-955198-23-3

Are You Happy

M.L.Ruscsak

Disclaimer

Although I do carry the title Doctor in front of my name, I do have to say I am not a licensed medical practitioner. However, I do have my PHD in Religious Studies. A master's degree in metaphysics.

Some of what I have degrees in may weave it's way into this books, but this is not about any one religion. This is a guide and nothing more . Use it as you see fit in order to build a better happier you.

This book in no way is a replacement for conventional therapy an should only be used as a tool and guide to finding a happier you.

Are You Happy

Dear Reader:
This book started out as a way to motivate and speak to a larger number of people about the things that I speak about everyday. However, books have a funny way of needing more and wanting to go their own direction.

So this is no longer that book you read to find inspiration and motivation. This is a tool to be used to better yourself. I do not ask anyone to reach out to me to discuss the worksheets. This is for the reader to get out of it what you put in.

With everything we do, creating a better you is work. It's being honest with ourselves. Being honest with our inner critic. And taking that first step to improve our lives.

There are great tools out there. This is only one of them.

Chapter One: We Say we are happy. But are we really?
Part 1: Negative Crutches
Chapter Two: I don't have the money.
Chapter Three: Relationships
Chapter Four: Our inner circle
Chapter Five: Homework
Part 2: What is holding you back from happiness
Chapter Six: The excuses we create
Chapter Seven: Getting rid of the excuses
Chapter Eight: Homework
Chapter Nine: Self Discovery
Part 3: Making it Happen
Chapter Ten: Make it happen
Chapter Eleven: The Power of Passion
Chapter Twelve: How to Become a Doer
Chapter Thirteen: Then Again…
Chapter Fourteen: How to Find the Drive, No Matter What
Chapter Fifteenth: Get a Washing Machine
Part 4: Unlock Your Brain's Hidden Potential
Chapter Sixteen: Unlock Your Brain's Hidden Potential
Chapter Seventeen: How Your Brain Function Can be Enhanced
Chapter Eighteen: How You Started Destroying Your Brain With Bad Nutrition and Stress
Chapter Nineteen: The Day You Stopped Learning
Chapter Twenty: The Solution
Part 5: The Power Of Your Subconscious Mind
Chapter Twenty One: The Power Of Your Subconscious Mind
Chapter Twenty Two: What is Visualization
Chapter Twenty Three: How can these techniques benefit you
Chapter Twenty Four: Changing your life though Visualization
Chapter Twenty Five: Recap

Part 6: Ways To Accelerate Your Gratitude

Part 7: Ways To Achieve a Positive Mindset
Chapter Twenty Six: Ways To Achieve a Positive Mindset
Chapter Twenty Seven: Tell Yourself You Can Do Whatever You Put Your Mind To
Chapter Twenty Eight: Stop Dwelling On The What- Ifs And Focus On The Present
Chapter Twenty Nine: Surround Yourself With Positive People
Chapter Thirty: Always Look At The Bright Side When Things Go Wrong
Chapter Thirty One: Other Thoughts

Part 8: The Proper Mindset For Health & Fitness
Chapter Thirty Two: Getting Started
Chapter Thirty Three: Why Do Most Health and Fitness Programs Fail?
Chapter Thirty Four: Determination and Motivation – Your Most Important Allies
Chapter Thirty Five: Selecting the Right Program
Chapter Thirty Six: Starting Slow
Chapter Thirty Seven: Target the Right Parts of the Body
Chapter Thirty Eight: Get Your Friends Involved
Chapter Thirty Nine: Chart Your Progress
Chapter Forty: Keep the Motivation On – Give Yourself Incentives
Chapter Forty One: Head to the Gym… Even if You Don't Want to
Chapter Forty Two: Ensuring You Stick to Your Health and Fitness Program
Chapter Forty Three: Final Thoughts

CHAPTER ONE

We Say we are happy. But are we really?

I was recently invited to talk to a group of individuals. It was to be an lifting promotion of great speakers. High energy. "If you do this you can be successful" kind of event. Now I love those events. We as the audience take in all of the positive energy. All of the words the speakers say and in that moment and we say to ourselves, "I'm really going to do this. I just paid over Three hundred dollars to be here. So I have to do it."

But then you have me. Sitting there in the audience because I don't want to be on stage yet. I want to gauge the room. I want to hear what the speakers are saying. Then again, I also what the audience to show me how to connect with them.

So it comes time for the organizer to call me to the stage. And this was told before hand that I would be in the audience not in the back. So She's not supersized to see me calmly coming up to the stage. My eyes never leaving hers. Yet there is no sense of urgency in my steps. No running and jumping. Yelling screaming. Trying to get the audience pumped up as so many speakers before me have done.

No that is not me. And will not do something that is not me. With this in mind I take the mic and gaze out to a sea of bodies looking dazed and confused. Some probably asking "who is she?" or "Is this some kind of joke?"

So I take a deep breath and ask, "By a show of hands who in the room is Happy?"

Of course Hands go up. And I look at this one woman way in the back. And this begins my case study.

As I call upon her to join me on stage. She obliges me.

"Thank you for joining me, may I have your name?"

She hesitates as she says, "Carol."

'Now Carol, we don't' know each other and we never met before this very moment. Correct?"

"Yes, that's correct."

I walk around the stage always careful never to turn my back fully to Carol. "Now you said that you are happy when I asked. But Why are you happy? What Makes you happy?"

"I have a wonderful husband. A decent job. I don't worry about my income. My kids are good. So yeah I'm happy."

'Ok great. Lets look at your job for a moment. You said you have a good job and don't worry about income. So what is your job."

Now note she said job. This is an important tell and you'll see why.

"Well I work as a paralegal. So the income is good."

"Ok, great. So you are good at research, managing clients, and book keeping. What about your boss. Do you like working for him?"

"He's a good person.So I guess so?"

"But are you happy to work for him?"

Now right here I have the audience's attention. But my friend whom I'm just met is getting uncomfortable. I'm not pushing her fr answers but she responds just the same.

"I'm happy to have a job if that's what you mean."

"Thank you. Lets talk about your family for just a moment. Your husband you've been together a long time?"

"About ten years."

Now you can't see it nor could my audience , but she's hiding something. The way her posture changed. Her eyes down cast. *"Oh that's great so I bet he's loving and supporting of your dreams and ambitions?"*

"Yeah, I guess?"

"So, you have some training in the legal field. And trust me when I say most paralegals know the law better than a lot of lawyers."

At that she laughs and nods. *"Yeah that is true. A paralegal has to know where to find all of the laws and loop holes to aid a lawyer in whatever case he or she has."*

"So, have you ever thought about taking you knowledge and going back to school to become a lawyer?"

"Well no, I…."

Now here I'll stop Carols' story. However, we will go over some of the key points that she raised.

She's viewing her job as a way to make money. Now there is nothing wrong with this. We all need to make ends meet. We ALL have to pay bills and keep a roof over our heads. So in that we all need our jobs. Yet, we also have to find our passion. In this case it was in the law. But for Carol and so many others we hold ourselves back. Letting the fear of not having money hold us back from our dreams.

Are You Happy

This is a crutch. So in life we have to ask ourselves first what makes us happy?

Then ask ourselves what is holding us back?

PART 1
Negative Crutches

CHAPTER TWO

I don't have the money.

Now I'm going to refer to Carol and her story as she is the prime example. Good job, long marriage, yet she still has dreams that are being held back.

Now I asked Carol about going back to school. Her answer is one I hear so many times. If I go back to school we won't have the income. Collage is expensive. It's too time consuming. And the list goes on. So lets break down the crutches.

We don't have the money.

Money is the biggest negative crutch out there. When our passion cost money to get started. Or when our dream needs money to be chased. We all go to the need of money first.

As money is the cause of our stress and what we repressive as happiness , it often becomes a double edge sword. One that cuts no matter what we do. So lets break this crutch.

If the first words that you think of is I don't have the money to… STOP. What do you have the money for? We know getting a degree in any college cost money but getting an education cost time.

Yes you read that right. Getting an education cost time not money.

The books that you need to get the education can more often than not be found in any library or on the internet for either free or less than a weeks worth of coffee.

But I need a degree to...

Ok, you're right. In may careers you need to have a piece of paper that says you went to some school and completed the classes. Guess what, there is no law that says the degrees has to come from a university or that it can't come from an online school. It only states you have to graduate.

So, that eighty thousand dollar bill for one year of college might now be less than thirty thousand for the full eighteen months it will take to do the degree program online.

But the degree from XYZ university is better than ...

Wrong. We as CEO's and those in positions to hire have for too long thought XYZ school is top of the line in education. And this is where you need to show us why you are the bast fit for the potion if we have two applicants with same work experience.

Don't use this a crutch. A degree is a degree so mater if the school is online or from university. It is the same knowledge from the same books. The only difference is the cost and the name of the school. Don't forget you still have a family to feed.

However, some of you may still be young enough not to have a family to support yet. So, how can you afford to get even on online degree? As we all know money is the biggest thing that keeps us from our dream.

For this we have a few choices.

First off join the military. Not only will you have the gateway to an education but you will also get real world experience. As a CEO, I will tell you any applicant that is coming from the military with an additional degree is more likely to get the position over someone from XYZ university. Why? They have already demonstrated they will not let something like money stand in their way from having the career that they want.

Now the military is not for anyone. And I get it. So, for you choice two. Work a day job and go to school at night. Your job today will give you the funds you need for tomorrow. It does not matter if you are working at a fast food place earning minim wage or in an entry level position in some company. There are ways for you to get that degree to better yourself.

Many places including our beloved fast food places have scholarships that you only need to inquire about. Depending on the place of employment they might offer to pay for ten to fifty percent of your schooling if you also remain with the company for a set amount of years after you graduate.

This is their return on the investment into your future. They do this not only to help you succeed but also to lower their turn over rate of new hires. This is beneficial arrangement for both you the employee and the company.

But I still need to pay...

Student loans and scholarships are there for any educational program you can think of. Student loans are the easiest to get as you are using your future career to pay for the loan but not paying for it till after you graduate. Now those who know money will tell you if you start paying on the loan before the first payment is due it will lower the amount you pay after the payment is due.

Scholarships. This is a bit more tricky and is not promised. It will require research and the ability to sell yourself to prove you are the best choice. And for the most part they will not pay one hundred percent of your college tuition, but they will pay something. And in money having something is better than having nothing.

But I won't have enough money to make ends meet….

For this I say to you. Are you sure or do you have a lifestyle that you won't be able to afford?

First off look at your monthly bills. What do you need verses what are you paying because you think you need? Rent/ mortgage,   power, heating/ cooling and food are what you need. Transportation is second. Now things that can be cut for the moment. Entertainment, how much tv do you really watch and is there a cheaper solution? Partying, vacations, shopping for new items that were not needed. These need to be set aside for the next five years.

Replace them with a side hustle. Something that cost little no nothing   to start that will bring in an addition income. This can be as simple as creating an app.

CHAPTER THREE
Relationships

Many women struggle with having the support of their families. However, this is something that is actually across the board. We have the perception that we have to be the bread winner, have dinner made by 6 o' clock, kids in bed, homework done. Whatever we were raised to believe.

Because I speak to more women than men this may seem more feminine. However, as more women are taking over key positions we are seeing men now fall into the same mindset. That said, lets start off with how we were raised.

I won't be home to support my family.

Support comes in a ll forms. Mentally, emotionally, physically and monetarily. So when I hear "I won't be there to support my family" I have ask, in what way will you not be there?

Lets take running the household first as that is the most common.

My children have to be up by a set time, be fed, put on the bus. The house needs cleaned. Dinner made. And the list goes on.

Ok great all of these are actions. How many people live in your household? How many people know how to cook, what chores can a child do? Are your children old enough to wake themselves up and go to school on time?

Children that watch their parent work and go to school will be more successful as adults. Why? They are given some responsibly early on. This can be getting up and grabbing a bowl of cereal before getting on the bus. To learning how to do the laundry, wash dishes and take care of the pets. The children that we teach to be self thinking and self motivated will be better than we are today.

Spouses and those we live with who are adults.

These are those we say we love. Those who think we will share our lives with. This means while we better ourselves they need to be the ones that help us along the way and not hold us back.

Someone that truly loves us will be there as we work and take the steps we need to follow our dreams. This may include them taking on a second job to make ends meet. It may mean helping with the kids and making dinner. If your response to will your love one support you in advancing your dreams is "I don't think so?" we have a problem.

Let's go back to our case study of Carol:

"If you went home tonight and told your husband of ten years you wanted to go back to school, what do you think he would say?"

"I can't ask.."

"Why? Why can't you ask?"

"he wouldn't support it. I know he wouldn't."

"You love him right? You've been happy for ten years? So why would he not be happy to see you happy?"

Now what Carol said had some points.

"He didn't want me working to start with."

We see this in household were one was raised with the mentality of there is a single breadwinner and the other should stay at home and raise the kids. This worked well pre- World War 1. However, since then the world has evolved, but the mentality has remained the same, passed down generation to generation.

So lets break this crutch.

A relationship no mater who the two partners are. they need to have the openness to talk to one another. If you can't talk about what makes you happy what are you talking about?

If your version of being happy is sitting on the couch reading a book and changing nothing about you or the life around you. Great, you found your bliss. However, if being at home and not aspirating to have a better tomorrow is how you see finding happiness then you need to have the conversation.

For many of us we find contentment in not changing. That is our comfort zone. We are with our partner because they came into our lives at a moment when we wanted the same thing. But as we stay with them our dreams change, they evolve. We want a new job, or a career. We want a better home or car. We want the things that require us to have a greater income to be able to afford those things.

Those who want us not to change or evolve will tell us wanting that new Tesla Plaid is a fools dreams. That we will never afford it. Or challenge us to how can you afford the car payment with our current income.Never once will they give us a solution to better ourselves.

Then there are those who see what we see within ourselves. Those are the voices we seldom hear but need to. They are the ones who say, ok you want this how do you plan to get it? What steps do you need in order to get that thing that will make you happy?

For me personally it was letting go of those who held me back. I had to break the chains that held me before I could see a path to what I wanted. A path that I started before I even understood what path I was on.

So now I ask you, What relationship is holding you back? And is it worth it?

Are you staying with what you know because you are comfortable? Or is that relationship one that will evolve with you?

Make notes here if you want. It is 100% in to write in this book.

_____
_____
_____
_____
_____
_____
_____
_____
_____
_____
_____
_____
_____

Are You Happy

Are You Happy

Are You Happy

Are You Happy

CHAPTER FOUR

Our inner circle

Let's be honest with ourselves for just a moment. We have three inner circles. We have our close friends who we think of as family. Our relatives who by blood we can trace our ancestry to. Then there is the third, this is called SELF.

There is not a single one of us who in some form has heard a parent, teacher, friend or some PSA on our television say, "Birds of a feather flock together." Ok it's safe to laugh, but the point is we all heard it. But what does that have to do with where we are in life?

Let's really look at our inner circles. Our friends, those who we talk to every day. Who we know when their children's birthdays are. They are in some ways closer than our family. So lets really look at them for a moment.

Friends come from everyday life, to work colleagues, school class mates,neighbors, or any other place that we might find out time doing something we enjoy. We tend to find friends with shared or common interest. This is where the birds of feather quote come in.

We have the mindset that we are drawn to a friend by a shared goal. Yet not all friends will be there as we grown and find our happy place. We have within our inner circle two kinds of friends. Those who will help us succeed and those whom will pull us back.

Now neither do this out spite but rather because of what they see in you. What you allow them to see of you. What mask do you wear when you speak to each group of friends?

But we are not yet ready to talk about SELF, but rather talk about your friends. In this case the negative crutch.

Think about this for a moment. You are having a group of friends over. Close friends that you have known almost forever. And the topic of conversation comes up on this wonderful idea you have. This idea could be anything from traveling someplace exotic to creating a business.

The first words out of your good friends mouth are , "Man, why do you want to do that for." The tone of the voice is enough for you to know this friend thinks it's a horrible idea. Now, the rest of your group is laughing about it because you have no knowledge of the subject. Don't have the funds. The education. Whatever the excuse is, you don't have it.

Stop. Really think right here, and reread that last part. How does that make you feel?

Like the most of us we will laugh it off. Yeah it was just an idea. Or you're right, I could never...

We take their words and let them stop us from going further. Our dream, our passion, the idea we just had because it would make us so happy, is now being stuffed to the back of our minds. Being placed in a box never to be realized.
There is an analogy to this. It's called crabs in a bucket. Everyone is trying to get out of the bucket but no one wants to let another get there first. Instead of helping, we pull them down.

Our inner circle of friends begin this pull, but it doesn't stop there.

We go to our relatives. With the same idea to get their opinions. And again they either are positive and supporting or will look you in the eye and tell you what you can't do. They will bring up dropping out of band. Or that School event that you just couldn't do. Bring up the things from your past that they know will keep you here in this moment.

It's not that they don't care about you but what mask do they see when they look at you? Are the adult ready to spread your wings? Or you the child that was in and out of trouble while in school?

With that we go into the hardest of our inner circles. The circle called SELF.

Now SELF has no one talk to. It has no outside influence. It is 100% what we say to ourselves when no one is around.

This is where your words have the most power. This is where we tell ourselves what makes us happy. What we can and cannot do. This is the place where we say what we want, what we dream, what we desire.

Are we when talking to SELF telling it, our friends are right? That our relatives are correct. Or are we standing the way because we are scared to move forward?

Let's do a case study.

Mike has had dreams of being an entertainer for years. He has done classes which his friends thought were a waist of time. Yet he did them. Put out his own content on his social media, where he gain some following.

After some time a friend comes to him, and says "Hay, I met someone today. You should give them a call. I don't know where it might lead. But you should check it out."

Now Mike has a few choices. Talk to friends and family who all know what he has been doing has not worked out. Take a leap of faith and make the call. Or talk to himself.

The conversation could go like this. "I've been doing this since school. I know I'm killing this but no one hears me. What can this fool do for me that I haven't already done? How does working with this person help me? They aren't big, so they don't know nothing. What makes them think they can help me?

Now the conversation can get darker from there. And often we will talk ourselves out of whatever it is. We will be the one to kill the dream faster than anyone from our inner circle ever can.

CHAPTER FIVE
Homework

Exercise One

What are the five things in your life that you would do today if you had the money to afford them?

1.)
2.)
3.)
4.)
5.)

Now what steps do you need to take in order to have the money to afford those five things? And be honest. Winning the lotto is not an answer.

_____
_____
_____
_____
_____
_____
_____
_____
_____
_____
_____
_____
_____
_____

Are You Happy

___

Exercise two

What five things do you want to tell your partner but "can't"?

1.)
2.)
3.)
4.)
5.)

What is stopping you?

___

Exercise three

Who is in your inner circle?

Of those closet to you, who tells you that you can't do something? And who are those who say you can?

Are You Happy

Are You Happy

PART 2
What is holding you back from happiness

CHAPTER SIX
The excuses we create

How many times have we tuned into a podcast, went to a conference, or spoken to a motivational speaker? Of those we have tuned into how many times have we followed thru on their advice?

It's ok to say in the moment of high energy, high engagement at some event to go "Yeah baby, I'm going to do this." Then when you get home or turn off the podcast to reconsider that choice.

It's ok. After all it's you're life, and it's up to you to know the best way forward. And truth is it may not be your time to move forward. But with help we will get you there so you will be ready.

However, this next part take work. Real work that no one but YOU can do.

Most of us use five our these most common excuses. Once we know what they are we can then overcome them.

1. I'm too old to start.
2. I'm not talented enough.
3. I wasn't born in the right area.
4. I come from a poor background.
5. I'm not smart enough.
6. I don't have the support.
7. I don't have enough time to discover what I like.
8. My family and friends don't think I'm capable.
9. I don't know if I will succeed.
10. I've already dedicated myself to a different path.
11. I'm just not lucky enough.
12. I didn't have the right teachers.

13. I'm not destined to succeed.
14. I'm not motivated enough.
15. I'm too easily distracted by other things.
16. I'm not educated enough.
17. I can't handle failure.
18. I will start tomorrow.
19. I'm not ready.
20. I don't believe I can do it.

However, before we can overcome a challenge we have to know what that challenge is for YOU. As each of us are different so is what our goal is.

So out of those Twenty negative thoughts what do you need to over come? It's ok to come back to this.

CHAPTER SEVEN
Getting rid of the excuses

Now that we have an idea of what the negative thoughts are, we can now look at them closely as every single one is made up in our own minds. Put there by our live experiences or by those our parents and grandparents have passed down to us.

I'm too old to start.

When working with people over the age of thirty I hear so many times "I'm too old to start...."

Says who? There is no exasperation date on when it is our time to accomplish something. This is a made up number created by society to keep people from finding their dreams. It does not in reality exist.

We have teens creating NTF businesses and Senior citizens creating small companies in Gas and Oil. There is no real timeline of when it's YOUR TIME.

True there are some things that need education first. Life experience. Even things that we need to put fear aside and just decide to create something. However, we can not expect to find our happiness by living by someone timeline that is not of our own making.

I'm not talented enough.
I wasn't born in the right area.
I come from a poor background

I block these three together as they are common "get out of doing it" excuses. We get some of this from our peers and from those around us. However, in truth it's excuses that work in every situation in order to get out of doing it. From trying out

for sports to running for a school office. Even as we get older and what to have a better job.
So lets debunk this here and now. Talent is created by practice. The more you practice something the better you become. From video games, to computer coding , to learning a second language. It takes time and practice.

Born in the right area and coming from a poor background are misnomer. There is no right or wrong area. There is born into a wealthy family or not. Most of today's business owners were not born wealthy. Don't believe me, pick up a copy of The Richest Man In The Trash Can by Antonio T. Smith Jr. Now I know his story as I consider him and his team great friends and mentors. He is a CEO of a multi million dollar company today, but he is one of several successful CEO's that started out with nothing.

Thus proving where you are is your mindset. It's up to you to decide where you want to be and how to get there.

Education

I'm not smart enough.
I didn't have the right teachers.
I'm not educated enough.

Education comes in all forms. It starts at home well before we enter school. Continues to the first thirteen years of formal schooling. Then Life takes over. We never stop learning. In truth we learn something everyday from those around us.

However it up to us to know what we know. It's up to us to decide what we learn. Personally I love history, however what is taught in school is a glossed overview of key points not every available fact. For that I had to take it upon myself to seek out facts. Including using a thing called a library that houses free books. Later adding tools like the internet and the history channel.

Always questioning what I was seeing and hearing to what I was reading and understanding.

This a practice we all must do no matter the subject matter. Teachers in school give key points. Keynote speakers give you... you guessed it key points on whatever they are speaking to.

It is always up to YOU to seek the information and learn what it is that you are passionate about.

Support
I don't have the support.
My family and friends don't think I'm capable.
I don't believe I can do it.

We spoke about this a bit prior to now. As your inner circle really does matter when wanting to get a head in life. But it starts with you. If **YOU** are not telling yourself that **YES I CAN**, then why would anyone get behind you? If **YOU** don't believe it then how will anyone else understand your vision.

Friends and family will alter their thoughts of you but not until you do so first. Then again, it may come down to removing them from your circle. Finding new friends that understand where you want to go. And showing you how to get there.

Procrastination
I don't have enough time to discover what I like.
I'm not motivated enough.
I'm too easily distracted by other things.
I will start tomorrow.
I'm not ready.

Are You Happy

Insert any excuse from above into either chart and you can see for yourself how our mind creates ways to get out of almost any situation . But one you understand this negative space then you can find a way to change it.

Procrastination Excuse	
The Truth	Old Unhelpful Conclusion
Answers to Disputation Questions	
End Result	
The Truth	New Helpful Conclusion

Approach Task/Goal
Unhelpful rules/assumptions are activated ⬇
Discomfort Driven

Detect Discomfort	Detest Discomfort	Dodge Discomfort

Procrastination Excuses ⬇
Procrastination Activities

Positive Consequences ⬇	Negative Consequences ⬇

Continue to Procrastinate

Being a procrastinator···	
How does it hurt me?	How does it help me?
If I change and no longer procrastinate···	

What will be good?	What will be bad?

Fear
I don't know if I will succeed.
I've already dedicated myself to a different path.
I'm just not lucky enough.
I'm not destined to succeed.
I can't handle failure.

There are several reasons fear stops us. We have the excuses that we say like above and those we never put words to.

THE "BIG FIVE"	

1. Fear of Failure	You cannot control other people's responses to your work; overvaluing these responses can create anxiety:
	  - Perfectionism: having unreachable standards will discourage you from pursuing a task
	  - Double Insurance: procrastination can be a way of protecting our self esteem
	  • ie. If I don't do well on an exam, it's because I

	didn't study, if I do well, I'm a genius because I didn't study
2. Fear of Success	Afraid of what might happen if we were successful
3. Fear of Losing Control	When feeling out of control, a person may develop a rebellious attitude in order to gain a greater sense of control. - ie. A professor wants an assignment in by a certain date, and I chose to submit it 2 weeks later
4. Fear of Separation	Afraid that successful completion of work could pull us away from others.
5. Fear of Attachment	Afraid that successful completion of work could draw others too close.

Now that we know our fears, and what is stopping us. Are you Ready to change? Are you ready to start the journey to take control of your life?

Are You Happy

CHAPTER EIGHT
Homework

Self Assessment Exercise:	
Physiological Symptoms of Stress	Map out on a Body Map; Where in your body do you feel the stress?
Irrational Thoughts	
Strategies & Ideas for Change	

Provide 5 or 6 answers for each of the following sentence
If I didn't procrastinate I . . .
If I didn't struggle with procrastination how would my life be different? What would I do differently?

If I stopped procrastinating what new problems or situations would I have to face that I don't have to contend with now?

Journal Exercise	
Your Fear of Failing:	- Identify alternate plans for success in case your original plan doesn't work - Use positive self-talk - Replace the thoughts which lead you to procrastinate with more healthy and productive ones (ie. I must···have to··· --I'd like to···choose to
The Tasks that you Avoid:	**Ask Yourself:** - What excuses do you use? - What were your thoughts and feelings? - What did you do instead of your work? - What was the outcome?
Your Worries and Self Doubts:	**Ask Yourself:** - What is the worst possible outcome? - What would I do if the worst happened?

	- What skills and strengths do I have that would help me cope? - How will I forgive myself for making a mistake?
Your Relational Fears:	**Ask Yourself:** - How do I feel about intimacy? - What are my intimacy boundaries? - How will I feel if my intimacy boundaries are crossed?
Helpful Strategies:	- Keep your work and play time separate - Schedule and make your playtime mandatory - Identify your unrealistic goals and replace them with more balanced and realistic ones - Practice relaxation exercises

CHAPTER NINE
Self Discovery

Learning ones SELF after hiding behind mask is one of the hardest things we all have to go thru. But where do we begin to learn ourselves? How do we even start?

First lets start off with some simple questions.

Self-awareness questions on values and life goals
1. What does your ideal "you" look like? 2. What kinds of dreams and goals do you have?
3. Why are these dreams or goals important?
4. What is keeping you from these dreams or goals?
5. Rank 5-10 of the most important things in your life in your career, family, relationships and love, money, etc. A. B. C. D. E.

6. Now think about the proportion of time you dedicate to each of these things.

7. What would you recommend to your children to do or not to do?

Self-awareness questions on personality

1. Describe yourself in three words.

   A.
   B.
   C.

1. Ask yourself if your personality has changed since childhood.

2. Is your personality like either of your parents?

3. What 5 qualities do you most admire in yourself?

   A.
   B.
   C.
   D.
   E.

4. What is your biggest weakness?

5. What is your biggest strength?
6. What things scare you?
7. Do you make decisions logically or intuitively?
8. How would you complete the question: "What if?".

Self-awareness questions on relationships

1. Describe your ideal intimate relationship. 2. How satisfied are you in your current relationship?
3. Who would you call if you only had a few minutes to live? What would you say?
4. Who have you loved the most?
5. Of all the relationships you have had, describe the best moment.
6. Describe a devastating moment in terms of

relationships.
7. Ask yourself if you treat yourself better than others?

SELF-AWARENESS HAPPINESS ASSESSMENT

WHAT TYPE OF PERSON ARE YOU TODAY?

DESCRIBE THE PERSON THAT YOU WANT TO BECOME ONLY USING THREE VERBS.
1.)
2.)
3.)

I AM HAPPIEST WHEN I:

Are You Happy

I AM MOST UNHAPPY WHEN:

PERSON THAT MAKE ME FEEL MOTIVATED AND INSPIRED.

THINGS THAT MAKE ME LAUGH.

THINGS THAT INSTANTLY PUT ME IN A GREAT MOOD

Now lets look at our core beliefs. Where did they come from? Were they passed down from our elders, or from our religion? Are they beliefs that make us a better person or do they cause us unneeded stress and unhappiness?

Step 1: Circle your top 10 values.

LIST OF GENERIC NEGATIVE AND POSITIVE BELIEFS	
Negative beliefs	Positive beliefs
RESPONSIBILITY/ I AM SOMETHING "WRONG" I don't deserve love. I am a bad person. I am terrible. I am worthless (inadequate). I am shameful. I am not lovable. I am not good enough. I deserve only bad things. I am permanently damaged. I am ugly (my body is hateful). I do not deserve . . . I am stupid (not smart enough). I am insignificant (unimportant). I am a disappointment. I deserve to die. I deserve to be miserable. I am different (don't belong)	I deserve love; I can have love. I am a good (loving) person. I am fine as I am. I am worthy; I am worthwhile. I am honorable. I am lovable. I am deserving (fine/okay). I deserve good things. I am (can be) healthy. I am fine (attractive/lovable). I can have (deserve) . . . I am intelligent (able to learn). I am significant (important). I am okay just the way I am. I deserve to live. I deserve to be happy. I am okay as I am.
RESPONSIBILITY/ I DID	

SOMETHING "WRONG" I should have done something. I did something wrong. I should have known better	I did the best I could. I learned (can learn) from it. I do the best I can (I can learn).
SAFETY/ VULNERABILITY I cannot be trusted. I cannot trust myself. I cannot trust my judgment. I cannot trust anyone. I cannot protect myself. I am in danger. It's not okay to feel (show) my emotions. I cannot stand up for myself. I cannot let it out.	I can be trusted. I can (learn to) trust myself. I can trust my judgment. I can choose whom to trust. I can (learn to) take care of myself. It's over; I am safe now. I can safely feel (show) my emotions. I can make my needs known. I can choose to let it out.
CONTROL/ CHOICE I am not in control. I am powerless (helpless). I am weak. I cannot get what I want. I am a failure (will fail). I cannot succeed. I have to be perfect (please everyone). I cannot stand it. I am inadequate. I cannot trust anyone.	I am now in control. I not have choices. I am strong. I can get what I want. I can succeed. I can succeed. I can be myself (make mistakes). I can handle it. I am capable. I can choose whom to trust.

Step 2: List them from 1 to 10 in order of importance. #1 is your top value in life.

Are You Happy

1.)
2.)
3.)
4.)
5.)
6.)
7.)
8.)
9.)
10.)

Core Beliefs
Please complete the statements below. Do not spend a long time thinking about them; simply write what comes into your head.
I am
Other people are
The world is

Now think about these three statements. How do they make you feel?

When did you first become aware of these beliefs?

Which experiences shaped them?

Who in your life may hold similar views?

Ask yourself: Do these beliefs still serve me? If not, which beliefs would be more constructive? Write down three beliefs about yourself, other people, and the world which you would like to cultivate going forward:

I am

Other people are

The world is

_____
_____
_____
_____

Identifying Your Negative Core Belief

Negative Self-Evaluations

- What do my negative self-evaluations say about me as a person?
_____
_____
_____

- What are the common themes, labels, words, or names I use to describe myself? What do they mean about me?
_____
_____
_____

- Do my negative self-evaluations remind me of criticisms I have received from others when I was young? What do those criticisms tell me about myself?
_____
_____
_____

- What things make me critical of myself? What do these things say about who I am?
_____
_____
_____

Negative Life Experiences:

- Did these experiences lead me to think there was something wrong with me in some way? If so, what was wrong?
_____
_____
_____

- Do I remember specific situations that accompany the negative thoughts or feelings I have about myself? What do my memories of these situations say about me as a person?
_____
_____
_____

- Can I link a specific person I know to the way I feel about myself? Has that person used certain words to describe me? What does their treatment of me say about me as a person?
_____
_____
_____

Biased Expectations:

- If my biased expectations were to come true, what would that mean about me as a person?
_____
_____
_____

- If I didn't avoid or escape or use my safety behaviors, what would I be worried about revealing to other people about who I am?
_____

_____
_____
_____

Difficulties Promoting Balanced Self-Evaluations:

• What made it difficult to think about myself kindly or treat myself kindly?
_____
_____
_____
_____

• What was I telling myself when I tried to do these things?
_____
_____
_____
_____

• What do my reactions to thinking/treating myself well tell me about how I see myself?
_____
_____
_____
_____

Perceived Outcomes Of Not Fulfilling The Rules

• If my rule was broken, then what would that mean about me?
_____
_____
_____
_____

Adjusting Negative Core Beliefs
Old Negative Core Belief I would like to Adjust

Rate how much I believe it (0-100%):			
Now:	When it is most convincing:	When it is least convincing:	Emotions

New Balanced Core Belief I would like to Adopt

Rate how much I believe it (0-100%):			
Now:	When it is most convincing:	When it is least convincing:	Emotions

Old Negative Core Belief

Evidence For	Alternative Ways of Looking at the Evidence

New Balanced Core Belief

_____ _____ _____	
Evidence For New Balanced Core Belief (from the past/present) _____ _____ _____ _____	Evidence For New Balanced Core Belief (what to look out for in the future) _____ _____ _____
New Behaviour/Experiments (things I can do to support or gain more evidence for my New Balanced Core Belief): _____ _____ _____ _____	
Rate how much I believe the following now (0-100%)	
Old Negative Core Belief:	New Balanced Core Belief

Are You Happy

PART 3
Making it Happen

CHAPTER TEN
Make it Happen

We all have goals we want to accomplish and things we want to make happen. Maybe it's your fitness you want to improve, maybe you're looking to enhance your career, or perhaps you have always envisioned a life of travel for yourself that you want to make a reality.

But while we all have goals, many of us lack the necessary skills and expertise to make those goals happen. This renders us somewhat powerless when it comes to choosing the trajectory of our lives. We're out of shape because we don't know how to stick to a training program, we're in jobs we aren't excited about because we don't know how to get out of our career ruts and we never seem to be able to get the money together to go travelling.

The worst part? When you tell someone how you're going to quit smoking, write a book or get into shape they just kind of… roll their eyes. And say 'sure'. And even we don't quite believe it…

It's time to change all that. Let's look at how to actually make it happen.

Positive Self-Talk Worksheet: Making It Happen

A little voice in our head gives us messages. Sometimes the messages say that we are clever and doing well. At other times they say that we are 'stupid' or that we can't do anything.

Write down how you feel when the messages are negative as well as how you feel when they are positive. The first has been done as an example.

You can also add some other situations to the list.

Other situations

Situation	Negative self-talk	Positive self-talk
Example: Speaking to someone new	I'm dull. They won't want to talk to me.	I'm interesting. Maybe I'll make a new friend.
Feelings	*Frightened*	*Excited*
1. Trying a new problem	I'll make a mistake.	The more I try the better I'll get.
Feelings		
2. Giving a talk to the class	They'll laugh and tease me.	I can do it.
Feelings		
3. Asking if you can join a game	They don't like me.	This will be fun.
Feelings		
4. Asking to borrow something special	They'll say no.	They'll say yes.
Feelings		
5. Giving an opinion	They'll all laugh.	They'll think I'm smart.
Feelings		
6. Making a speech	I'll make a fool of myself.	I'll do a pretty good job.
Feelings		
Situation	**Negative self-talk**	**Positive self-talk**
7.		
Feelings		
8.		
Feelings		
9.		
Feelings		

10.		
Feelings		
11.		
Feelings		

Positive Self-Talk Worksheet: Nothing Ventured, Nothing Gained

Some people don't try new things because they're scared.

1. What would be the worst thing that could happen if you didn't do as well as you would like at:

   Learning pottery? _____

   Reading aloud? _____

   Surfing? _____

   Trying a new hairstyle? _____

   Introducing yourself to someone new? _____

   Learning the piano? _____

2. List some additional activities you could try and give the worst and best things that could happen.

I should try	The worst that could happen	The best that could happen

3. The messages we give ourselves are called 'self-talk'. Give four examples of negative self-talk that could make you feel frightened of trying something new.

a. _____

b. _____

c. _____

d. _____

   Now give the positive self-talk that should replace these negative messages.

a. _____

b. _____

c. _____

d. _____

Positive Self-Talk : The Inner Voice

Being a positive learner is about the language you use when you talk to yourself.

We have three internal voices – the YES voice, the NO voice, and the I DON'T KNOW voice.

As a human being, you have an inner world and an outer world.

Your inner world is made up from your thoughts and your feelings (plus a lot of physical things, like your spinal cord, heart, intestines, lungs, etc).

Your outer world is made up of the other things – other people, buildings, circumstances, family, the weather, your outer environment.

Within your inner world there is a voice – this is your Inner Voice of thought.

Our Inner Voices talk to us in certain ways. Sometimes they talk to us in a YES voice, sometimes in a NO voice and sometimes in an I DON'T KNOW voice.

The great news for learning and living is that we can program our Inner Voice and become the voice and the person we wish to be. What we say with our Inner Voice will show up as 'living' to the Outer World people.

This is great news, because it means our Inner Voice is powerful.

It means you are powerful.

The more you choose to program a YES voice, the more powerful you will be!

Positive Self-Talk Worksheet: Being A 'Yes' Person

What makes a 'Yes' person?

Yes	No	I don't know

I've got this task to do: YES I'll give it my best shot!	No, I can't do it!	I don't know.
I will be able to do this.	This is silly, this is stupid.	I'm not sure
There is a solution and I'll find it.	I can't do this: it's too hard.	I think I'll try!
I'll do it now!	I'll do it tomorrow (next week).	I could do it tomorrow.
Sounds good, I'll give it a go.	I'm hopeless. This is impossible: I'm not even going to try!	I don't know about that. Maybe I'll wait and see.
I can do it, it may take time and effort but I can do it!	I'm dumb.	I could but I've got a cold.
Yes, I made that mistake and I can learn from the experience.	It's not my fault, don't blame me (it is their fault ... teachers, parents, boss).	Don't ask me!
That person has some really good points.	I don't like that person.	I'm not sure. I'll wait to see how they match up.
I'm good at ... (maths, reading).	I'm hopeless at ...	I'm not really good at anything.
I am a learner.	They'll laugh at me.	I'm tired.
I am good value.	I'm no good.	I am not sure of myself.

So, what makes a YES person?

- YES people have a YES physiology. A YES body language is confident and happy.

- A YES face is open and smiles a lot.

- YES people look for possibilities and not restrictions.

- YES people see problems as learning and seek solutions rather than being stuck in the problem.

- YES people celebrate themselves and others.

Are You Happy

- YES people program their Inner Voices for YES living.

- YES people communicate clearly and openly.

YES people stretch their thinking and train their brains

Are You Happy

CHAPTER ELEVEN
The Power of Passion

First we need to discuss in detail how to come up with a fool-proof plan to accomplish any goal. We need to create a simple formula that can be applied to any kind of goal and pretty much any set of circumstances and then we go ahead and do just that: applying it to fitness goals, relationship plans, travel plans and more. There, you'll learn how to word goals in such a way that you become more likely to stick at them like glue. You learn how to make plans that let you achieve things you never thought possible and you learn how to find what it is you want.

In this guide, we're going to take a different strategy. Here, we're going to talk about how you stick at those goals. We're going to discuss how you keep going for the things you want, even when you've had an exhausting day in the office, even when you've got a serious migraine, even when things just don't seem to be going your way…

It starts with passion…

Find Your Passion and it All Falls Into Place

Finding your passion is not only the secret to happiness but also the secret to success and to becoming the kind of inspiring, charismatic and magnetic person you've probably always wanted to be.

When I think about someone who is driven, passionate and motivated, my mind will often turn to Dwayne 'The Rock' Johnson. This is someone who has perhaps the best physique in Hollywood right now and looks like a real-life action hero. On top of that, he's a guy who is one of the highest paid in the industry, who has already conquered the world of sports, who has become a social media mogul... who is even tipped to become president one day!

So that's a lot of achievement for one guy and when you follow him on Instagram or watch him on YouTube, it's easy to see how he's gotten to where he is. The Rock is simply brimming with passion and excitement at all times. He clearly absolutely loves what he does and you can see it even in his smile.

The Rock is highly charismatic, which is what makes him such a successful actor and so great to watch. But this charisma is a result of him loving what he does – it makes him walk differently, talk differently and gives him a full, genuine smile. Studies show that we rate people as more charismatic if they gesticulate more. And guess what makes you gesticulate more? Passion. Passion makes us speak with our whole body because we truly believe what we're saying and because we're so excited to share that information.

And it's undoubtedly that passion that also allows the Rock to wake up at 4am in the morning to work out. If you follow him on Instagram, this is what a huge number of his pictures are showing: his alarm going off at 4am before he hits the gym.

Can you imagine someone like the Rock coming home from a day at work and looking tired and defeated? He never does: because what he does is so intrinsically motivating to him.

The first thing you need to do then is to find that passion and find the thing that you really want to do. That's what will give you the unstoppable iron determination to keep at your goals no matter what.

And finding your passion means being brutally honest with yourself. It means that you reject the things that other people want you to do. You forget the things that you believe you're supposed to want to do and instead you focus on what you really want to do. Likewise, you need to think about what you're going to enjoy working toward. It's not enough to want the end result: you need to be happy putting in the work every day to get there too.

In other words, you can't just want to get strong, you need to enjoy going to the gym. Don't want to write a book, learn to love writing.

When you find the thing that really brings you to life, you'll find it is MUCH easier to stick at it. In fact, you may well find that it is everything else that falls by the wayside!

Journal activity

What stirs you and makes you feel alive?

We all feel it, something building up inside us when we see or experience a situation; an urge to do something about it. I am sure there have been occasions in life when something has evoked strong feelings from you. Often, these are tied to your passion. Take time to look back and pen down what caused it. I know these answers won't come to you in a single day, but after much introspection, you will be able to recollect it all.

_____
_____
_____
_____
_____
_____
_____
_____

What activity makes you lose track of time?

Think about those activities that you really enjoy doing and long to keep doing. Activities where you get so immersed that time simply fly by – jot them down.

Are You Happy

What makes you cry?

We humans are highly emotional beings, even though many claim otherwise. We cry when we are sad, happy and when we are emotionally touched. The situations or things that make us cry are often about things we are passionate about. So crying is a big indicator! What touched you so deeply that you cried recently?

Are You Happy

People often take their 'natural knacks' or gifts for granted; however the skills that are easiest for us can provide a good clue to areas we are most passionate about. People have a tendency to assume that just because something is easy for them, that it is easy per se'! Others may find the same tasks difficult – largely because their heart is not in it or they do not have the same strengths and skills.

What skills and talents come easily/most naturally to you? Which ones give you a buzz or a huge sense of personal satisfaction?

Are You Happy

What strengths do others notice and admire?

Are You Happy

What changes could you make to bring about constructive changes?

Are You Happy

What fascinates you?

Passion goes in all directions. It can be as tangible as a job or a car or a house, or as intangible as a dream or an idea. You could be passionate about anything.

Work	Hobby
Sports or pastime	Family
An idea	A cause
A belief	The environment
Travel	Other cultures
The past	The future
Films	Books
Music	Collecting things
Gardening	Making money

What captures your interest and attention? List as many things as you can that you could be/are passionate about.

_____
_____
_____
_____
_____
_____
_____
_____
_____
_____
_____
_____
_____

Are You Happy

CHAPTER TWELVE
How to Become a Doer

Once you find the thing that you're really excited about, you need to devise a plan to make that happen and then stick with it. This is what will make you a doer and not a talker or a dreamer. We are not truly defined by our intentions, our aims, or our ideals. In reality, we are defined by our actions and these are what will make us successful or otherwise.

You want people to stop rolling their eyes when you tell them about your plans and instead to be a person who carries real weight and gravitas when you explain your plans. When you say you're going to travel around the world, you want people to know that that is really going to happen.

But actually, one of the ways you do that is to stop telling people at all. Why? Because according to some studies, telling people your dreams and plans is actually one of the surest ways to ensure they don't happen.

And why is that? Well for starters, it suggests that you're looking for external validation. Remember what we said about your passion being intrinsically motivating? That means that simply engaging in that activity or working toward that goal should be enough. You shouldn't need a reward and you certainly shouldn't need accolades from others.

If you're really fascinated with your book project, then you should be quite happy to work on that project in your spare time without ever needing to tell anyone about it! This is a much more powerful form of motivation and drive than anything you can get from people telling you that they think you've done a great job!

The other problem with telling people your plans is that it creates a 'psychic release' of sorts. That sounds crazy I know but what I mean by this, is that it gives you a sense of reward and relief. More to the point, telling someone your plans actually means that you can adopt those plans as part of your identity even before anything has happened.

So for instance, if your goal is to quit smoking, then you might feel a great sense of reward just by telling people that you're planning on quitting smoking. That is to say, that you tell someone you're going to stop smoking and then suddenly, you feel as though you're already not a smoker anymore. People will praise you and tell you 'well done' even before you've actually quit and you'll feel safe in the knowledge that other people now know that you don't want to be a smoker. It sounds crazy but this can then remove the incentive to actually quit! You've already got the sense of reward, so you don't need to put the effort in!

Personal Story:

I started writing I think it was my third book when I started telling people I was writing it. Family members -- blood recitatives-- told me I wasn't an author, or a writer.

I started the doing my radio show, again the eye rolls from those that should have been supportive.

All of these self thoughts of how proud they would be and moment they were less than thrilled was a huge blow.but it was the eye rolls when I mentioned starting something new I had to step back and ask myself who am I doing this for?

Am I writing a book, going back to school, starting a company, or the half a dozen other things that I have grown to do, for me or am I doing it for someone else? Am I doing something that makes me happy and that I find joy in or am I looking for something else; for someone else?

It was the moment that defined the difference between doing for someone else, and doing what makes me happy. It became the moment when I decided I would writer for me and not tell people what I'm doing. If I travel I'll post pictures of where I'm at but not why. Unless it's a work thing of course.

But the point is I found my why, I found my happiness. Now is it time for you to find the difference between when to tell people what you did -vs- what you plan on doing.

Are You Happy

CHAPTER THIRTEEN
Then Again...

But then again, there are scenarios where it does to pay people, or at least to tell some people.

And there are two reasons that this can be the case.

The first is that telling people can help you to feel as though you have stakes. When you tell someone you plan on losing weight for example, you then know that they're watching you and waiting to see if you actually achieve your goals. This can create a social pressure that actually can be very helpful in motivating you along.

And you can actually make this even more the case by encouraging people to call you on your actions. Get a friend to watch you and make sure you are sticking to your goals and doing what you said. They can monitor your performance and if you don't do what you said you'd do, you could even get them to somehow enact a form of punishment. Tim Ferriss recommends getting a friend to donate your money to a charity that you don't like if you don't achieve your goals. That's some powerful motivation right there!

The other reason is that telling people can mean you have a partner in crime. This is sometimes actually a requirement, while in other cases, it will be a very useful asset.

The scenarios where it is actually necessary to tell someone about your plans tend to pertain to your relationships. That is to say, that if you're in a relationship with someone and your hope is to go travelling or to spend money on the hoes, then you're going to need to get them on board before you go ahead.

But even where you don't need them to agree, it can help a great deal to have your partner along for the ride. This is particularly true when it comes to dieting. One of the hardest parts of sticking to a diet is often the social aspect and this comes from our relationships a lot. If you're married or in a long-term relationships, then no doubt you will spend evenings eating pizza in front of the TV, you'll share a box of indulgent chocolates from time to time, or you'll go out for romantic meals.

When you've decided to go 'no carb', it is a lot harder to have a romantic meal. And it's a lot harder to enjoy pizza in front of the TV too. This is why having your partner along for the ride can make all the difference as this way, the diet becomes something you can do together, rather than something that you are doing that may seem unsociable.

Better yet is finding a gym buddy. A gym buddy is someone who can come along on your workouts, help to spot you through the heavy lifts and give you encouragement and motivation as you're running. This can make a big difference to your motivation and make the whole experience of going to the gym a lot more enjoyable. Moreover, when you have a gym buddy, you have someone that you don't want to disappoint. If you skip a session, then you'll be leaving them in the lurch and that creates extra pressure to go. Likewise, there will be times when they are feeling low and you help to pull them through.

And better again then that is finding people who are as passionate as you about a business idea. If you can find people to go into business with and you all truly believe that your idea has real potential – that it is something that could change the world or at least make you a lot of money – then you're going to find that the passion and excitement in your group becomes contagious and that everyone in the group helps to buoy and excite everyone else. This can be a great feeling and it is something that all of the very best startup companies have in common. It's a state that is often referred to as a state of 'flow' and it's what you feel when you're so impassioned about something that you become highly focussed and it's all that all of you can talk about and think about.

So what's the real scoop here? Should you tell people your plans or not?

Well, that depends on how you do it and the nature of your plans. It's a great idea to tell people your goals if you are looking for a partner. If you think you can get other people excited about what you're doing and get other people on your side, then speak to people and get them excited. What you mustn't do though, is tell everyone how you're going to be rich, famous or well-travelled – as that is very likely to make you much more of a talker than a doer.

- Look closely at your close friends. Who Supports you and has these characteristics :
- An Active Listener
- An active listener doesn't offer advice unless you ask them for it nor do they make the conversation about themselves or their issues.
- Empathy
- Someone who can feel what you're feeling either because they've experienced your problems themselves or because they're very tuned in.
- Trusted
- They need to be trustworthy and have the integrity to keep your conversations between the two of you.
- Nonjudgmental
- They shouldn't assign blame when hearing your stories. Instead, they should be capable of understanding that we're all human and that we all make mistakes.
- Authentic

- ➤ Someone who allows their own emotions and vulnerabilities to show through without any pretense.
- ➤ Self-Aware
- ➤ Being self-aware allows a person to better empathize with others.
- ➤ Calm
- ➤ They need to be your rock; they can't be prone to emotional or dramatic outbursts, or they could make things worse.
- ➤ Perceptive
- ➤ Someone who can see the forest for the trees when you're too emotional to be able to.
- ➤ Patient
- ➤ Someone who can listen for hours at a time or can offer their time without the need to constantly interject their opinion.
- ➤ Optimistic
- ➤ They need to have an uplifting outlook on life and give you the strength to keep going.

CHAPTER FOURTEEN
How to Find the Drive, No Matter What

Another important tip is to always keep in mind the 'why' behind what you're doing. Too often, we work toward a goal in a blind manner having forgotten the real reason we're doing it. You know you want to get into shape and that means that you need to train for half an hour 4 times a week.

But you don't keep that in mind during the actual training. Instead, you just hit the gym, grumble about it and then push your way through the gruelling workouts.

What you need to do instead, is to focus your mind on the reason you're training and to really feel the emotion that drove you to want it in the first place. This is where visualization can come in handy.

For instance, if it's getting into shape that you're interested in, then you need to think about why you want that and what it's going to feel like for you to be in the shape you want to be in.

Many people want to be in great shape because they want to look and feel good about themselves. They want to fill out a suit, they want to attract members of the opposite sex (or same sex), they want to feel powerful and they want to wake up with tons of energy and vitality every morning.

To find the will to train, you need to remember that each workout is a stepping stone to that end destination. So close your eyes and picture it: picture being highly muscular, or lean. Picture looking great and turning heads for all the right reasons. Picture putting on a top and knowing it looks amazing on you.

You can also use visualization in other ways. One good one is to picture the alternative. Imagine what will happen if you keep putting your goals off. Maybe you end up working in the same dead-end job for the rest of your life. Maybe you get fat and flabby and lose all of the hard work you've already put into your physique.

I also like to encourage myself to see the situation as a challenge and I do this in a similar way by visualizing defeat. I imagine that I'm exhausted, depressed and far too crushed to train. And then I ask myself if I want to take that, or if I want to get up and kick ass. The tireder you are, the harder it is to work at your goals, the more ass you can kick!

Activity

I don't want to do _____. But if I do _____, then I will see a significant financial payoff both now and in the future and will feel good about my choices.

I don't want to do _____. But if I get _____ done, then it will make my boss happy and lower my anxiety every time I have a one-on-one meeting.

I don't want to do _____. But if I make progress on _____, then I will have so much less stress next week and be prepared for _____.

ASK WHY FIVE TIMES.

You want to start running. You want to exercise regularly. You want to lose weight and feel great.

But why? Why is this goal important to you? Why does it matter?

A good exercise is to insert your goal and your reason into the following sentence:

I want to _____ because _____

For example, I want to run a 10k because it will help me get into shape.

Then, insert the reason into the first part of the sentence and repeat the process over and over again. For example:

- ✧ I want to get into shape because I don't have enough energy to be productive at work.
- ✧ I want to be productive at work because it's important to provide for my family.
- ✧ I want to provide for my family because being a great parent is rewarding.
- ✧ I want to be an amazing parent because I believe it's part of leading a good life.

Set goals, use the table on the next page as a template.

Are You Happy

Lessons					
Completed?					
Timed					
Relative					
Attainable?					
Measurable?					
Specific					
When by?					
How?					
Why?					
Type					
Goal					
Date					

CHAPTER FIFTEENTH
Get a Washing Machine

Get a Washing Machine

And while you're at it…

Get a washing machine.

Okay, that might seem pretty random but it's going to help you in a lot of cases and more to the point, it is a good example of a mindset shift that can really make a difference.

The point is that when you really know your passion and when you know what is truly important to you, then you should know what you want to do with your time and with your life. And that means you need to think about restructuring your lifestyle so that you are spending less time doing the things you don't want to do.

In other words, once you know what your passion is and you know how you want to be spending your time, you can then structure your life around that thing and that means removing the unnecessary distractions. Distractions like washing dishes.

If you really want to accomplish your goals, then it makes sense to design your life around them. Change the way you spend your time on a day-to-day basis and remove the time-consuming activities that don't take you closer toward your goal. You don't need to spend ages washing dishes and likewise, if you can shorten your commute then you can spend more time on your goal as well.

You can also make your goal easier to accomplish by making the steps easier. If you want to work out regularly for instance, then it may help a great deal to stop going to the gym and to instead train from home. This way, you're now removing a time-consuming journey and creating a situation where you can easily squeeze in a quick routine when you get home from work, or first thing in the morning before you set off.

All these steps and techniques should help you to become better at sticking with your goals and finding the will when the going gets tough. Set yourself up for success, remind yourself why you're doing the things you're doing and get people on your team.

And if it still isn't working? Then you might need to reassess the nature of your goal and the strategy you're using to get there. That's where the Make It Happen workbook comes in, so check that out and let's make it happen!

Of course there is nothing like one on one coaching sessions. Those should only be sought when you are really ready to change your mindset.

PART 4
Unlock Your Brain's Hidden Potential

CHAPTER SIXTEEN
Unlock Your Brain's Hidden Potential

Your Short Guide to Ultimate Brain Health

Your brain is just like any other part of your body. In order to maintain optimum function and to get the very most from it, you need to treat it right.

And this is rather important, seeing as your brain is responsible for pretty much everything you do. Whether it's the obviously 'mental' stuff, like concentrating at work or performing complex sums; whether it's physical stuff like regulating your breathing, helping you sleep and directing your movements; or whether it's managing your emotions and helping you to feel happy and calm.

Whatever it is you're doing or experiencing; your brain is at the route of it. And thus, you can improve every aspect of the human experience just by focusing on your brain health.

CHAPTER SEVENTEEN
How Your Brain Function Can be Enhanced

The trouble is that many people have very little idea just how to go about looking after their brains. This is the most previous piece of equipment in the world – more powerful than infinite supercomputers – but we tend to just ignore it and hope it all works out okay.

In fact, a lot of the time, we unintentionally subject it to a fair amount of abuse!

For starters, most of us eat entirely the wrong diet and this means our body doesn't have access to the raw materials it needs in order to maintain optimum brain function. In the short term, this makes us feel groggy and slow but in the long term, it can lead to cumulative damage that results in neurological diseases and age-related cognitive decline. That's right: it's not inevitable that you should become forgetful and cantankerous as you get older!

The other problem is that most of us don't use our brains enough. We don't challenge them, and we don't train them. Due to a phenomenon called 'brain plasticity', it is actually possible for us to train and grow our brains just like a muscle. New neurons can be created, and new connections can be formed and strengthened. This all means that it's possible for us to develop certain brain areas beyond others and actually enhance our abilities as a result.

But when you stop challenging your brain or training it, it can lead to all kinds of problems. Especially when you combine that with high levels of stress and the aforementioned poor diet...

Are You Happy

Before we go further let's do somethings that are fun and can help get your brain healthier.

Fun Activity

Directions: Using the code breaker below, decipher each scrambled sentence and record how long it takes you to the nearest second using a clock or timer. Then answer the questions that follow.

Code Breaker

A = Z   E = V   I = R   M = N
Q = J   U = F   Y = B

B = Y   F = U   J = Q   N = M
R = I   V = E   Z = A

C = X   G = T   K = P   O = L
S = H   W = D

D = W   H = S   L = O   P = K
T = G   X = C

1. Vcvixrhv   hgivmtgsvmh blfi   ylwb zmw rnkilevh   blfi nrmw.

_____   _____ ____ ____ _____   ____ ____.

Time it took to solve: _____

2. Ksbhrxzo   zxgrergb   kilwfxvh   kilgvrmh   gszg   rnkilev nvnlib.

_____   _____   _____   _____ ___   ____   _____ _____.

Time it took to solve: _____

3. Vcvixrhv kilwfxvh z yizrm xsvnrxzo gszg rnkilevh nllw.

_____ _____ _ _____ _____
__ ____ _____
____.

Time it took to solve: _____

Think It Through:

1. You were likely able to decode the third sentence more quickly than the first one. What was your difference in seconds?

2. If you were able to solve the third sentence more quickly, why do you think that was so?

3. Write the following sentence using the coding key above: "I am a super decoder." Were you able to write some of the words in code without looking at the key?

4. How can you use this knowledge of how your brain works to improve your life?

5. How can you use this knowledge to improve your ability to stop and think before making a decision?

Yes this activity was around while we were in school. So why do it now? As we age we need to always challenge your mind by learning harder things.

10 Quick Brain Exercises You Can Do Right Now

1. Add up the alphabet
Give the different letters of the alphabet the numerical values 1–26 (A=1, B=2, etc.). Try to think of words in which the sum of the letters is 40 (or 45, 50 etc).

2. Study the phone bill
Take a look at your phone bill and try to recall to whom each phone call was made. If you rely on your cell-phone full-time now, look back at your recent call log and try to remember what you and the other person spoke about.

3. Mess with your mouse
Flip your computer mouse, so that moving the ball left and up makes the cursor move right and down. Or, work your non-dominant hand by plugging the mouse into the opposite side of the computer.

4. Reminisce
Try to recall the names of teachers or fellow students in your class at school. See if you can remember details such as what they wore or what kind of person they were. Next time, think about a past workplace or a street where you once lived. You will be surprised at how much you can remember.

This Is my favorite and something I started doing in school more out of need than out of desire but it proves to be a neat trick that not everyone can do, only because they choose not to learn.

5. Read upside down
Turn a book or a newspaper upside down. Read the page from the bottom to the top. Notice how much more effort is

needed to make sense of the structure of sentences. Can you find the missing word in this tricky brain teaser?

6. Test your vocab
Write down as many words as you can starting with a certain letter of the alphabet in 2 minutes. Try letters such as M, T, and C or challenge yourself with O or Y.

7. Clock yourself
Concentrate on the second hand of a watch or clock for 1 minute. Now close your eyes and see if you can time a minute exactly. You might be surprised how off you are.

8. Take a new route
Driving, running, or biking the same way every day allows your brain to go on autopilot. Stimulate your mind by trying a new route. You'll have to visualize the roads in your head, which activates to cortex and the hippocampus.

9. Memorize a picture
Look at a photo online and try to remember everything that appears in it. Cover the photo and list those things. Now look at the photo again and see how many you got correct.

10. Eat with chopsticks
Similar to switching up your computer mouse, this one forces you to slow down and take in what's happening. As a bonus, doing this will help you savor your food even more.

Are You Happy

needed to make sense of the structure of sentences. Can you find the missing word in this tricky brain teaser?

5. Test your vocab.
Write down as many words as you can starting with a certain letter of the alphabet in 2 minutes. Try letters such as M, T, and C, or challenge yourself with C, or Y.

7. Clock yourself.
Concentrate on the second hand of a watch or clock for 1 minute. Now close your eyes and see if you can time a minute exactly. You might be surprised how off you are.

8. Take a new route.
Driving, running, or biking the same route every day allows your brain to go on autopilot. Stimulate your mind by trying a new route. You'll know you're visualize the roads in your head, which activates the cortex and the hippocampus.

9. Memorize a picture.
Look at a photo as long as try to remember everything that appears in it. Cover the picture and list those things. Now look at the photo again and see how many you got correct.

10. Eat with chopsticks.
Similar to switching up your computer mouse, this challenges you to slow down and take in what's happening. As a bonus, doing this will help you savor your food even more.

120

CHAPTER EIGHTEEN
How You Started Destroying Your Brain With Bad Nutrition and Stress

The way that most people eat these days is enough to severely damage our health and lead to serious problems.

As mentioned previously, the brain needs a large number of very specific nutrients in order to function well. These include the all-important precursors to various neurotransmitters. Neurotransmitters are chemicals that change our mood and the way they think – they help us to sleep, to feel good, to focus and to remember things.

But the brain makes these neurotransmitters out of vitamins, minerals and amino acids. If you aren't getting enough l-tyrosine for instance, then you might struggle to make dopamine – the neurotransmitter responsible for helping us to focus, stay motivated and remember things. Meanwhile, tryptophan is what the brain uses to create the 'feel good' neurotransmitter serotonin. This is then later converted to melatonin to help us sleep.

Vitamin B6 is a building block for numerous neurotransmitters including dopamine, epinephrine (focus), serotonin and GABA (calmness). Choline, found in eggs, is the precursor to acetylcholine which can improve pretty much every single aspect of your cognitive function!

Then there are the countless other crucial nutrients that the brain needs to perform optimally. For example, healthy arbs are what fuel the brain with energy, antioxidants protect the brain cells from free radicals and zinc enhances brain plasticity.

But most of us are not getting anywhere near enough nutrients in our diets. That's because we eat far too much 'processed foods. Processed foods contain lots of calories to make us feel full, but they are 'empty calories' that are devoid of the things we need.

Meanwhile, our switch to a more modern diet that doesn't include things like fish, mean that even those who try to eat 'healthily' are generally not getting the things they need. A perfect example of this is the modern lack of omega 3 fatty acid. Omega 3 is a fatty acid found in fish (and some plants), which aids with 'cell membrane permeability' (especially the DHA form). This is important because it allows things to pass more easily through the cell walls – good things like nutrients and signals from other parts of the body. At the same time, omega 3 fatty acid is also used by the brain to create a number of hormones that are linked with managing the blood. This way, omega 3 is able to reduce blood pressure and heart problems.

Most importantly though, this also allows omega 3 fatty acid to reduce inflammation in the brain and the predominance of 'pro-inflammatory cytokines. This is highly important, seeing as pro-inflammatory cytokines are what make you feel so groggy and confused when you're poorly or very tired. Brain fog is a serious problem and it's made worse by the fact that most of us also have far too much omega 6 fatty acid. Omega 6 fatty acid is a useful nutrient in its own right but when we get too much of it, it can actually lower omega 3 and cause more inflammation. Most of us have far too much omega 6, because it is used in all kinds of preservative oils.

This is then combined with chronic dehydration, which most of us experience on a daily basis. Dehydration can also cause inflammation in the brain, while also generally leading to sluggish performance.

These processed foods are also exampling of 'simple carbs' – carbs that have no sustenance and which the body processes very quickly. This results in a sudden spike in blood sugar that provides you with a burst of energy, followed by an immediate trough straight afterward.

Then there are all the toxins and high quantities of sugars that we consume regularly – and the cancer causing free-radicals.

Is it any wonder that you struggle to think through the thick haze sometimes?

The Role of Stress

Even worse is the role of stress. Today, it's a sad fact that a great number of us experience chronic stress, leading to elevated levels of cortisol (the stress hormone) in our systems. This has a number of serious negative effects on our health and on our brain function in particular.

For starters, when there is excess cortisol in the system, this increases the amount of the neurotransmitter 'glutamate'. Glutamate is a general excitatory neurotransmitter, and this means that you'll experience increased brain activity across the board. This leads to heightened awareness and that sense of nagging thoughts. It also makes it harder to sleep, which can lead to memory loss and depression. But perhaps the most worrying side effect is that ongoing stress also leads to the creation of more free radicals – unattached oxygen molecules that attack the brain cells and potentially cause cancer. It can also generally destroy brain cells, robbing you of your ability to think straight.

Also worrying is that stress depletes levels of brain-derived neurotrophic factor (BDNF). This is the principle neurotransmitter that stimulates the creation of new brain cells and it's highly important for increasing brain plasticity. In other words, stress prevents you from learning and this in turn is associated with depression, OCD, schizophrenia, dementia and Alzheimer's disease.

And cortisol also acts contrary to numerous other important neurochemicals. That is to say that when cortisol goes up, these go down. And key victims here are serotonin (happiness), testosterone (drive) and dopamine (motivation and learning).

Just in case that you thought the 'more alert' part sounded cool earlier. Note that this also increases your awareness of things like nagging pains, irritating noises and more. This is why stress is associated with tinnitus – the ringing sound some people experience in their ear that has no cause.

And meanwhile, heightened stress can actually cause our frontal cortex – the part used for planning, creativity and higher-order thinking – to completely shut down.

So, in short, stress can absolutely neuter your cognitive ability in the short term and cause long term damage if it is allowed to continue.

Foods for a healthy brain:

Green, leafy vegetables. Leafy greens such as kale, spinach, collards, and broccoli are rich in brain-healthy nutrients like vitamin K, lutein, folate, and beta carotene. Research suggests these plant-based foods may help slow cognitive decline.

Fatty fish. Fatty fish are abundant sources of omega-3 fatty acids, healthy unsaturated fats that have been linked to lower blood levels of beta-amyloid—the protein that forms damaging clumps in the brains of people with Alzheimer's disease. Try to eat fish at least twice a week, but choose varieties that are low in mercury, such as salmon, cod, canned light tuna, and pollack. If you're not a fan of fish, ask your doctor about taking an omega-3 supplement, or choose terrestrial omega-3 sources such as flaxseeds, avocados, and walnuts.

Berries. Flavonoids, the natural plant pigments that give berries their brilliant hues, also help improve memory, research shows. A study done by researchers at Harvard's Brigham and Women's Hospital found that women who consumed two or more servings of strawberries and blueberries each week delayed memory decline by up to two-and-a-half years.

Tea and coffee. The caffeine in your morning cup of coffee or tea might offer more than just a short-term concentration boost. In a 2014 study published in The Journal of Nutrition, participants with higher caffeine consumption scored better on tests of mental function. Caffeine might also help solidify new memories, according to other research. Investigators at Johns Hopkins University asked participants to study a series of images and then take either a placebo or a 200-milligram caffeine tablet. More members of the caffeine group were able to correctly identify the images on the following day.

Walnuts. Nuts are excellent sources of protein and healthy fats, and one type of nut in particular might also improve memory. A 2015 study from UCLA linked higher walnut consumption to improved cognitive test scores. Walnuts are high in a type of omega-3 fatty acid called alpha-linolenic acid (ALA). Diets rich in ALA and other omega-3 fatty acids have been linked to lower blood pressure and cleaner arteries. That's good for both the heart and brain.

Not everything when finding what makes you happy is hard work and drastic change. Sometimes it is delightful culinary experience. Here are some tasty recipes to try.

One-pan salmon with roast asparagus

Ingredients
400g new potato, halved if large
2 tbsp olive oil
8 asparagus spears, trimmed and halved
2 handfuls cherry tomatoes
1 tbsp balsamic vinegar
2 salmon fillets, about 140g/5oz each
handful basil leaves

STEP 1
Heat oven to 220C/fan 200C/gas 7. Tip the potatoes and 1 tbsp of olive oil into an ovenproof dish, then roast the potatoes for 20 mins until starting to brown. Toss the asparagus in with the potatoes, then return to the oven for 15 mins.

STEP 2
Throw in the cherry tomatoes and vinegar and nestle the salmon amongst the vegetables. Drizzle with the remaining oil and return to the oven for a final 10-15 mins until the salmon is cooked. Scatter over the basil leaves and serve everything scooped straight from the dish.

Salmon & spinach with tartare cream

Ingredients
1 tsp sunflower or vegetable oil
2 skinless salmon fillets
250g bag spinach
2 tbsp reduced-fat crème fraîche
juice ½ lemon
1 tsp caper, drained

2 tbsp flat-leaf parsley, chopped
lemon wedges, to serve

STEP 1
Heat the oil in a pan, season the salmon on both sides, then fry for 4 mins each side until golden and the flesh flakes easily. Leave to rest on a plate while you cook the spinach.

STEP 2
Tip the leaves into the hot pan, season well, then cover and leave to wilt for 1 min, stirring once or twice. Spoon the spinach onto plates, then top with the salmon. Gently heat the crème fraîche in the pan with a squeeze of the lemon juice, the capers and parsley, then season to taste. Be careful not to let it boil. Spoon the sauce over the fish, then serve with lemon wedges.

Spiced lamb kebabs with pea & herb couscous

Ingredients
400g lean lamb shoulder, cut into 3cm cubes
1 tsp ground cumin
½ tsp cayenne pepper
1 tsp sweet smoked paprika
1 tbsp olive oil
24 cherry tomatoes
140g couscous
400ml hot vegetable stock
140g frozen pea
1 large carrot , coarsely grated
small pack coriander , chopped
small pack mint , chopped
juice 1 lemon
2 tbsp extra virgin olive oil

STEP 1

Soak 6 wooden skewers in water for 30 mins (this prevents them burning when cooking on the griddle or barbecue). Put the lamb cubes in a large bowl with the spices and olive oil. Toss everything together well and season.

STEP 2
Thread a piece of lamb onto a skewer, followed by a cherry tomato. Repeat, adding about 4 pieces of lamb and 4 cherry tomatoes to each skewer, until all are used up.

STEP 3
Meanwhile, put the couscous in a large bowl, pour over the hot vegetable stock and add the peas. Stir, then cover with cling film and leave to soak, about 5 mins.

STEP 4
Heat a griddle pan. When all the liquid has soaked into the couscous, gently fluff up the grains using a fork, and stir in the carrot, herbs, lemon juice and olive oil. Mix everything together well, season and set aside.

STEP 5
Place the skewers on the hot griddle pan and cook for 5-6 mins, then turn and cook for a further 5-6 mins until the meat and tomatoes are charred and cooked through. Serve the skewers with the couscous.

Spicy yogurt chicken

Ingredients
8 skinless chicken drumsticks
142ml pot natural yogurt
1 tsp chilli powder
1 tbsp ground cumin
1 tbsp ground coriander
2 tsp ground turmeric

STEP 1
With a sharp knife, make a few slashes in each drumstick. Mix the remaining ingredients in a bowl, season to taste. Add the drumsticks, rubbing the mixture well into the meat. If you have time, cover and chill for 30 mins.

STEP 2
Remove the drumsticks from the marinade, shaking off the excess. Cook them on the barbecue for 20-25 mins, turning occasionally, until cooked through.

Pear & blueberry breakfast bowl

Ingredients
1 firm but ripe red-skinned pear, unpeeled
2 tbsp oats
150g pot 0% fat bio-yogurt
3 tbsp skimmed milk, plus a bit extra
1 tbsp pumpkin seeds
2 handfuls blueberries

STEP 1
Grate the pear into a bowl and add the oats, half the yogurt, the milk and most of the seeds. Leave for 5-10 mins, then check the consistency and dilute with a little more milk or water if it is too thick. Spoon on the remaining yogurt, pile on the berries and remaining seeds, then serve.

Breakfast smoothie

Ingredients
1 small ripe banana
about 140g blackberries, blueberries, raspberries or strawberries (or use a mix), plus extra to serve
apple juice or mineral water, optional
runny honey, to serve

STEP 1

Slice the banana into your blender or food processor and add the berries of your choice. Whizz until smooth. With the blades whirring, pour in juice or water to make the consistency you like. Toss a few extra fruits on top, drizzle with honey and serve.

Broccoli & sage pasta

ngredients
140g quick-cook spaghetti
140g long-stem broccoli , trimmed and cut into 5cm lengths
3 tbsp olive oil
2 shallots , sliced
1 garlic clove , finely chopped
¼ tsp crushed chillies
12 sage leaves, shredded
grated parmesan (or vegetarian alternative), to serve (optional)

STEP 1
Boil the spaghetti for 1 min. Add the broccoli and cook for 4 mins more.

STEP 2
Meanwhile, heat the oil in a frying pan and add the shallots and garlic. Gently cook for 5 mins until golden. Add the chillies and sage to the pan and gently cook for 2 mins. Drain the pasta, mix with the shallot mixture in the pan, then scatter with Parmesan, if you like.

CHAPTER NINETEEN
The Day You Stopped Learning

All this would be bad enough, if our current lifestyles didn't also involve so little learning and actually using our brains.

The brain is a tool that has one singular interest: Helping us to survive in our environment. And the way it does this is to adapt and to evolve, to enable us to get more reward and less punishment. It helps us seek out food, shelter and sex, while avoiding pain, hunger and fear.

To do this, our brain needs to learn. It predicts outcomes, tries new things and then decides whether or not to do that again based on the response. If it got food, then the neural connections involved in that action are strengthened and it will do it again in future. If it got pain, then the neural connections will be largely overridden, and it won't do it again...

But the brain loves doing this. Learning, exploring and adventuring keeps the brain youthful and nimble and encourages continued growth and the production of more dopamine and BDNF to encourage plasticity.

Once life stops being unique and interesting, the brain stops needing to pay attention and can rely on existing connections. Thus, the things you are already good at get strengthened and everything else gets pruned. You become set in your ways and your brain ceases production of dopamine and BDNF – preventing you from being able to learn new things. And this is when dementia has been shown to kick in.

Now with all this in mind, consider the way your life has changed from when you were younger to now. When you were born, everything was new, and your brain was highly plastic. You were constantly learning new things and discovering new things. Thus, your brain was filled with novelty and it responded to this by producing huge amounts of dopamine and BDNF. This is why children can pick up languages so incredibly quickly. It's why they're always smiling and it's why they're always curious and learning.

As we get older, we become more familiar with the world around us. Things get more set-in stone and we no longer have to learn simple things like how to walk or what a tree is.

But we're still learning – we're learning at school; we're learning when we watch TV and we're daydreaming about all the things we could be! This continues to a lesser extent into adolescence as we head off to college and as we start dating for the first time, learn to drive and learn to pay the rent in our own apartments.

Even in young adulthood, much is new as we travel with friends and as we try out different jobs and progress through our careers.

But then things start to slow down. We stop learning new things and we find a job that we like and stay in it. Meanwhile, our bodies become tired and we gain more responsibilities – like children and mortgages. We settle down in some part of town and don't move home or environment…

The result is that we end up stuck in a rut and going through the same motions day in, day out. All the while our brain is flooded with stress hormones and we're eating entirely the wrong diet.

All this contributes to a general slowing of our brain function, damage to our mood and well-being and the growing inability to learn. This is why older people are stereotypical more closed minded – they're literally become set in their way. It's like taking the same route across a lawn every single day –

eventually that route will become entrenched and you'll never be able to go any other way.

Brain cells start dying, your mood deteriorates, and you crawl toward inevitable old age.

Are You Happy

CHAPTER TWENTY
The Solution

Wow, that's depressing! The good news is that it's also wrong.

The inevitable bit, that is. Old age may be inevitable, but the cognitive decline associated with it most assuredly is not. In fact, there are plenty of ways you can combat age related cognitive decline and keep your brain youthful and healthy well into older age.

Read on and we'll look at what some of the things you can do are...

Fix Your Nutrition

Step number one is to fix your nutrition. Instead of eating lots of processed foods, sugary snacks and preserved ready meals, you need to switch to nutrient dense sources of complex, slow-release carbs, to lean proteins, to vegetables and fruits!

This doesn't mean switching to some kind of fad diet. It just means eating food with real, natural ingredients. And it means seeking out those 'superfoods' whenever you can.

If you only add a few things to your diet, consider these:

Eggs

Eggs are absolutely amazing in just about every way when it comes to your brain and your health in general. For starters, eggs are one of the only 'complete' sources of protein. This means that they contain 100% of the essential amino acids that you can't produce in your body, thereby helping you to produce all kinds of neurotransmitters.

Eggs are also rich sources of selenium, vitamin D, B6, B12, zinc, iron and copper… all things that can boost your brain power.

Best of all, eggs are also high in choline – which is the chemical precursor to 'acetylcholine'. Acetylcholine meanwhile is a neurotransmitter that helps keep us alert, awake and highly attuned to our senses.

As though that wasn't enough, eggs are a great source of saturated fats. Saturated fats are also highly beneficial for the brain, seeing as the brain is largely made of fat. Plus, it boosts testosterone, which is linked with drive and motivation, as well as mood (and low cortisol).

Tuna

Tuna is an excellent source of amino acids yet again and is nice and lean for those of you trying to keep their weight down. What's more, is that tuna is a brilliant natural source of omega 3 fatty acid. We've already seen the amazing health benefits of omega 3 fatty acid, so 'nuff said on that front. Oh, and it's cheap too!

But while tuna is great source of all these things, it is a little high in mercury owing to pollution – so don't eat more than a small can a day.

Red Grapes

Red grapes are high in a substance called resveratrol. Resveratrol is a potent antioxidant, which means that it can prevent the action of free radicals in the brain and thereby reduce your chances of brain tumor or Alzheimer's. At the same time though, resveratrol is also able to enhance the function of the mitochondria, thereby helping them to produce more energy for your brain cells. It turns out that resveratrol isn't quite as powerful as some earlier studies suggested but it's certainly still no slouch either!

Coconut Oil

Coconut oil contains something called MCT oil – Medium Chain Triglycerides. This is a type of oil that stimulates the liver to produce ketones. Ketones meanwhile are an alternative energy source that the brain can use instead of glucose. The brain actually prefers ketones for a number of tasks, which makes this a great way to give your

Supplements

If you want to give your brain a little more edge, then you can do so by seeking out a number of different supplements and nootropics. Some good examples include:

Creatine

Creatine allows the body to recycle its ATP stores. ATP is the body's primary source of energy and is used by every single cell – including the brain cells. This way, creatine is able to give us more energy to think smarter and improve mental vigilance. It has been shown in studies to increase IQ.

Omega 3

Getting omega 3 from the diet alone can be hard, so supplementing with a DHA product is a good choice. Avoid cod liver oil if you're pregnant however, due to the large amounts of retinol.

Caffeine

Caffeine will give you a short-term boost in concentration, memory and wakefulness. It's not perfect and can decrease creativity while also being mildly addictive. But it is neuroprotective and can prevent Alzheimer's.

Lifestyle Changes

Finally, don't forget the power of numerous lifestyle changes. Getting better sleep is absolutely critical to increase neurotransmitter stores, remove adenosine (which contributes to brain fog) and strengthen new neural pathways.

Also, very important is exercise. The brain is primarily designed for movement – this is what the majority of brain areas actually specialize in! Moving the body is the best way to learn and to stimulate plasticity, while cardio will also improve circulation to the brain while adding a short-term increase in serotonin and endorphins.

Finally, make sure to keep learning, keep exposing yourself to novel surrounds and keep trying new things. Computer games are actually a great way to do this – as every new game includes new environments and new rules to uncover!

Of course, we're only just scratching the surface of what you can do to increase your IQ, your wakefulness, your creativity and your long-term brain health. In the full book, we go into much more depth discussing the huge number of specific brain training techniques, health strategies and more that you can use to start getting more out of your brain and looking after it.

A lot of this is about what you need to stop doing. And it's about making small changes to your routine and lifestyle – like eating a little more fruit and perhaps walking a little more. Doing small things can make a huge difference to the way you feel now and, in the future,, it could potentially be the difference that adds 5 or 10 years of quality life. Look after your brain and everything will get better.

PART 5
The Power Of Your Subconscious Mind

CHAPTER TWENTY ONE
The Power Of Your Subconscious Mind

In today's modern age, it seems that everyone is focused on their successes and consumed by their failures. A lot of people have a hard time finding the balance, and need a little extra help to get out of their negative thoughts so that they can begin to find the inspiration that they need to achieve their goals. Visualization techniques are an incredible tool that allow us to harness the power of our subconscious minds in a way that allows us to attract more opportunities to ourselves and recognize the resources and tools that we already have at our disposal.

Visualization is an important step in a long process of achieving our goals. When we are able to fully encapsulate our personal power, then there is nothing that can get in our ways. We become unstoppable people who are not going to take no for an answer. We will stay motivated to take the steps that need to be taken for us to succeed, and we can become extremely well-versed in helping other people to achieve their own goals through the experience of mastering our own minds and emotions in a productive way.

If you have ever wondered how visualization can work for you, then you won't find a better guide for you than the Beginner's Guide to Visualization. This is a book that goes into detail about the ways that visualization has become a prevalent and effective method for achieving our goals and it even gives some history on where the practice came from and how you can best use it to serve your own life.

Overall, this is a process that could change your life, and equipping yourself with the knowledge necessary will help you to take the steps you might not have even known you need to take in order to realize your potential and fulfill your dreams!

What's Holding Me Back?

Ahh, challenges. Everybody has them. Everybody. In this chapter, you will learn the tools that you can take with you throughout your life to overcome obstacles as they come up. And they will come up. Life has ups and downs – that's what makes it life. Some days will be good, and some will be not so good, but overall, it's about how you handle these challenges. Your Thoughts Govern Your Life Thoughts are running through our head every day. The brain is the beginning of creation, giving birth to new ideas thousands of times per hour and also creating everything in your environment. Your thoughts are powerful – so powerful in fact that they have the ability to lift you up or tear you down. When you give in to other people's ideas and thoughts, you give up your power. Other people's beliefs can now lift you up or bring you down.

Example: Suppose I said to you the following:
What's the matter with you? You aren't that smart. You don't have the education you need. What makes you think that you can get to the next level?
How does that make you feel inside?

_____
_____
_____
_____
_____
_____
_____

Now suppose I said this:
You are terrific. You know, the most successful people aren't really all that smart, but they know how to get the education that they need to take it to the next level. Even if you don't

know exactly what needs to be done, you are taking action and that's great. I believe in you.

How does that make you feel inside?
_____
_____
_____
_____
_____

Can you feel the negative and positive energy in those statements?
Concentrate on where you feel that energy in your body. Often, negative energy will show up as a "gut feeling" or a heavy heart, and positive energy will feel light and airy. Notice how these things work in your body – it will be a very good indicator of intuition and a decision barometer in the future. Your mind always knows what is right for you and you will receive signs in the form of feelings in your body. Listen to these signs and you will not make mistakes.

Your Personal Choices, Decisions and Subconscious Mind
YOU ALWAYS HAVE A CHOICE. No matter what the circumstances, situation or issue at hand, there are always at least two choices that can be made. Think hard about this when you have the need to say, "well, I didn't have a choice". Name a situation where you felt you didn't have a choice:
_____
_____
_____
_____
_____
_____

Now, knowing that you DO have a choice, what could you have done (or do, if the situation presents itself again) to honor your right to choose?

___

Making the Decision for Achievement

Successful people make a decision to have success. They don't leave it to chance. They make personal choices that are in line with their value systems, their goals and their own personal truths. They break through limiting beliefs and realize that there is always a choice.

Before you can move forward, you must make a decision to have success. This comes in very big and very small ways in your life. Notice I did not say "how" it will come to you, but you must give yourself the permission and the willingness to do whatever it takes to achieve your goals. Be open to alternate routes – there is a much larger force at work to help you and you don't know all there is to know. Right now, we are going to write our own personal statement of decision to have success. Put it on a piece of paper and tape it to your mirror if you have to.

I, _____ have made the decision to have the success in my life that I deserve and set out to achieve. I will meet obstacles head-on and choose to get through them in
whatever way is necessary. I let go of my need to control the details and I allow myself to focus on the end result of my goal, knowing that I am meant to be successful
in my endeavors. Practice in everyday life. Start with small decisions, like getting a parking space in the front of the mall...

What's Holding You Back?
You were meant to be successful, but maybe you're not exactly in the place you'd like to be financially, personally or professionally. Let's examine the beliefs, fears, doubts and self esteem issues that really hold us back in that area.

Your Money Beliefs
Take a few minutes and examine your beliefs in this area: On a scale of 1-5, with 1 being disagree and 5 being totally agree, rate the following statements:

____Rich people are greedy
____I may be poor, but at least I'm honest
____Money is evil
____I don't have enough money
____There isn't enough money to go around
____Money is hard to manage
____If I'm rich, then my friends won't like me
____It's righteous to be poor
____It's not about the money
____"Money doesn't grow on trees"

Your Personal Doubts
___ I'm too _____
___ I'm not _____
___ I'm not good enough
___ I'm not ready
___ I'm not smart
___ I don't know how to do it

Knowing what you know now about the subconscious mind, think hard about what these beliefs are sending to your subconscious mind and how your subconscious mind is making sure that your beliefs come true!
Examining Your Beliefs and Doubts
From the exercise above, take your biggest money blocker and your biggest personal blocker and write them here:

My Biggest Negative Money Belief _____
_____
_____
_____
_____
_____
_____
_____
_____
_____

My Biggest Personal Doubt _____
_____
_____
_____
_____
_____
_____
_____

Where did these come from? SOMEONE GAVE YOU THESE BELIEFS! Who? Let's examine a bit further. Did your negative belief come from your parents, teacher, aunt, uncle, sister, brother, other loved one?

My Biggest Negative Money Belief came from:
_____
_____
_____
_____
_____
_____
_____
_____

My Biggest Personal Doubt came from:
_____
_____
_____
_____
_____
_____
_____
_____
_____
_____

YOU DO NOT HAVE TO ACCEPT SOMEONE ELSE'S BELIEFS!

Breaking Through Fear

Fear is a real and important part of our lives. It can be one of the most exhilarating or scary parts of our life mission. Fear exists to keep us safe. Basic fears, such as the fear of falling or fear of loud noises, are there at birth. They are the self-preservation mechanisms in place so that we don't jump off buildings to see what flying feels like.
But fear can also manifest terrible situations in our imagination and hold us back from achieving what we really want in life. That's right – we are holding OURSELVES back – nobody else is doing it for you!

Let's examine some common fears: Put a check mark next to the fears you've already identified in yourself.
___ Fear of Failure
___ Fear of the Unknown ("what if")
___ Fear of Rejection
___ Fear of Success
___ Fear of Humiliation or Ridicule
___ Fear of Loss
___ Fear of Making a Mistake
___ Fear of Losing Control

I have a very simple, 3 step process to discover and deal with your fears.

Determine the EXACT source of the fear.

Ask yourself – is this really my TRUTH right now or am I making it all up?

Take action in small steps
Determine the exact source of the fear

When dealing with a fear, just like dealing with a goal, you first need to brainstorm with yourself, no matter how silly it seems. Write down your secret thoughts, the ones you worry about.

My situation surrounding my biggest fear is:

_____
_____
_____
_____
_____
_____
_____
_____
_____
_____
_____
_____

Ask yourself, is this the TRUTH or am I making it all up?

_____
_____
_____
_____
_____
_____
_____
_____
_____
_____
_____
_____

What actions can I take to continue on my path and push past my fear?

_____
_____
_____
_____
_____
_____
_____
_____
_____
_____

CHAPTER TWENTY TWO
What is Visualization

So what is visualization and how can it work for you? This is a good question. Visualization is the act of presenting physical images and thoughts and words of affirmation to your brain so that it can focus on the goal you have set in place. When the brain is focused on these things, it will subconsciously begin to guide us toward opportunities beyond our imagination. It will work while we are sleeping or doing other things to help us and lead us in the direction of the successful completion of the goals that we have set for ourselves.

Visualization is a strategy that many successful people have implemented in order to stay focused on their goals and to create a life of abundance. Athletes are able to use visualization to enhance their performance, writers can use it to meet deadlines and build whole new worlds for their audience, and business people are able to use it to create successful plans and partnerships. Data visualization is a way to incorporate numbers into images that are easier to understand and process, and using these graphs and charts, people are able to make information comprehensive and digestible in a way that enhances productivity and that encourages employees to continue putting their best foot forward in their projects.

Visualization is the act of putting thoughts and ideas in a format that uses pictures and positive thinking to see the successful completion of your goals. It is showing your mind what your objective is and letting it use its tremendous power of observation and problem-solving to help us move forward. It has been in use for centuries, and without it, it is likely that language and communication as we know it wouldn't even exist.

So you can see just how important this strategy could be. It has accomplished tremendous things for the human race, and it can accomplish tremendous things for you personally, too! The Beginner's Guide to Visualization can show you how!

CHAPTER TWENTY THREE
How can these techniques benefit you

Visualization techniques have been around for centuries, and there are multiple ways that they can benefit us. By utilizing the power of our subconscious mind, we are able to keep our minds focused on achieving our goals. If we have a vision board, for example, it is a visual reminder to the brain of what we are working toward. It can prevent us from feeling discouraged and help us to remember that what we want to achieve is going to happen for us. All we have to do is keep taking the steps forward!

All the time, our mind is making connections. But when we are focused on the negative aspects of our lives, the connections our minds make are not productive. In fact, they create neural pathways in the brain that can cause us to spiral in and out of depression and encourage us to wallow in negativity. And when we are focused on negativity, that is what we will attract into our lives. This can hold us back and cause untold issues in our lives and relationships. If we can't focus on the good, then only more bad is to come.

This can be combatted by learning more about the negativity bias. As mentioned in The Beginner's Guide to Visualization, overcoming the negativity bias is one of the most important things that you can do to create a successful visualization technique. You have to truly believe that you are capable of achieving the goal that you are setting for yourself. That way, you continue to put the work in and you don't lose your motivation to move forward.

All that forward momentum will only be enhanced by visualization techniques. These techniques give our brains a solid goal and vision to focus on so that when we encounter resources and tools and opportunities in our own lives that will help us to move forward and achieve our goals, we will recognize them for what they are. We won't overlook these chances and we will be better equipped to seize the day. However, when the negativity bias is working against us, we may be too discouraged and distraught to trust our own perception and these opportunities may pass us by. That's the last thing we need, and visualization techniques can help us to stay focused on the positive and allow us to create room in our lives for more of the same.

Ultimately, visualization techniques can help us to turn our minds into our best friends and most valuable asset in achieving our goals. By knowing what to focus on, our subconscious will never stop working to help us accomplish the things that we most desire. And in the process, we will gain confidence in ourselves and an understanding of exactly what it takes to create and maintain the lifestyle we most desire! The choice is up to you.

CHAPTER TWENTY FOUR
Changing your life though Visualization

The Beginner's Guide to Visualization outlines all of the specific techniques that you can use in order to make visualization work best for you. It goes in depth about the power of vision boards, affirmations, a good daily routine, and how important it is for us to believe that we will achieve our goals. No ifs, ands, or buts. We will achieve them.

Of course we all have obstacles in our course, and The Beginner's Guide to Visualization is aware of those as well. It touches on how to most easily change your life and benefit from visualization by removing the biases in your life and surrounding yourself with positive an uplifting people who want to see you succeed. If you are surrounded by negative people and naysayers, it can be so much more difficult to believe in yourself and to allow yourself to believe that you will one day be in the position you most desire.

Overall, the visualization techniques that are outlined can help anyone who is struggling. No matter where you are on your path, The Beginner's Guide to Visualization has some insight for you. Beginner, intermediate, or expert, you will benefit from visualization techniques and they will change your life for the better. Life as we know it will never change overnight, but we can take the steps that we need to take to make sure we are living with a positive mindset, and enhancing our daily lives to the fullest extent possible.

No matter where you may be on the path toward your goal, visualization techniques will help you to stay motivated and to encourage you never to give up. And when we believe that we have the power to succeed, then ultimately we have no choice but to succeed.

The power of our unconscious minds is right at our fingertips. Instead of letting yourself become bogged down by your own discouragement and a lack of belief in yourself, use these techniques to help you learn and grow and become comfortable with your own path. Avoid the discouragement of negative thinking and remember that you are capable. And then, show your mind the picture of the life you want and let your mind help you get there! Use the law of attraction to live in abundance and change your life!

CHAPTER TWENTY FIVE
Recap

Everybody has a hard time staying positive at some point in their lives. We can all take our failures and mistakes pretty hard, especially if we don't have a positive support network. When we grow up feeling powerless in our own lives and feeling as if we don't actually have control over our destinies, then it can be incredibly difficult for us to overcome that and truly believe that we are capable of achieving our dreams and goals.

Fortunately, The Beginner's Guide to Visualization can help you to overcome these discouraging thoughts and help you to stay focused on all the different ways that you can become the person you have always wanted to be. All of us are capable of achieving our goals, no matter how many times we may make mistakes. The key is to stay the course and learn what techniques work best for you and what isn't as beneficial.

Fortunately, visualization techniques are backed up by science and have been encouraged by some of the most successful people in the world. Our brains are powerful enough to affect our bodies just with our imaginations, so why not utilize that power to help us achieve the things that are the most important to us? We have every right to take part in the world's abundance. Let The Beginner's Guide to Visualization show you how!

Starting today, you could begin to transform your life. You can set the goals you may have been too afraid to set before, and you can train your brain to work in your favor as you move throughout your life. Allow your subconscious mind to harness the power you need to seize the opportunities that will allow you to succeed. Anybody can do it, and millions of people already have! So what's the harm in trying?

Vision boards, affirmations, and careful selection of the things that you allow into your life and allow to affect you, are all ways that you can begin right this moment to change your life forever. If you can see a better future for yourself, then you can have that future. All you have to do is take the first steps. If that sounds like a good deal, and it really is, then The Beginner's Guide to Visualization is the book for you. Use the powerful, scientifically proven visualization techniques to help you to take your life back into your own hands and reclaim your own power. The only person who can do it is you, so start down on the path today!

PART 6
Ways To Accelerate Your Gratitude

CHAPTER TWENTY SIX
Ways To Accelerate Your Gratitude

There are so many benefits to living a life of gratitude. It will make you much more optimistic about your future and it will help you to attract more good things in your life. There are physical and mental health benefits as well. Practicing gratitude regularly will strengthen your immune system and help you to cope better with stress.

If you are committed to making the transition to a gratitude filled life then the 12 powerful and effective methods in this special report will help you to achieve your goal a lot faster than other methods. They are all simple to implement and very effective so don't just read this short report – take action every day.

Consistency is the most important thing when you are trying to develop a gratitude habit in your life. You need to use these methods even if you don't feel like using them. It is going to take at least 30 days for a new habit to form so that you start doing these things automatically. So learn, implement and keep implementing!

In the mornings when you get up grab your gratitude journal and write down three things that you are really grateful for in your life right now. These can be small things or big things – it really doesn't matter. So for example the fact that you woke up and you have another day to look forward to is a good reason to be grateful.

As you write each one down think about the reason why you are so grateful and experience how this makes you feel. So if you are grateful to have a specific person in your life then write down why they are so important to you and the feelings that you have about them.

Repeat this process before you go to bed each night. It will help you to sleep a lot better because you will lay your head down feeling happy and content with your life. So go through the "three things" process at the start and end of each day to really accelerate your gratitude.

It is really easy for you to perform an act of kindness for others every day. An act of kindness can be something small such as giving someone praise or encouragement. You can start with your family. Provide some help to them in some way. You need to change your mindset to look for ways that you can perform small acts of kindness each day.

If you work in an office think about who has helped you recently. Write them a note thanking them for their help and mention the specific thing that they helped you with. You should always say "thank you" to people with sincerity when they do something for you. But this is not enough as a thank you is expected as the norm.

You will get a lot of satisfaction from helping others even in a small way. When you perform your daily act of kindness, note the reaction from the receiver of this act. It is very likely that their face will light up and they will say some very nice things to you. This will make you feel warm inside and inspire you to keep going with your gratitude.

There is good all around you – all you need to do is look for it. In the summertime notice the butterflies that are dancing around the flowers in your backyard or in the park. Look at the people that you live with and think about how proud you are of all of them.

Most people live a very fast paced life these days and take most things for granted. They don't pause and take the time to appreciate the world that they live in and the people that are in their life. If you are not currently doing this then don't worry. It is really easy to take a few seconds out of your busy life and just focus on the smaller things.

Leading a life of gratitude is all about being appreciative of what you already have. So schedule a time each day where you will just take a little time to look around you and reflect on your life. You will soon discover many things that you can be grateful for.

People spend too much time dwelling in their past and concerning themselves about their future. What has happened in the past is gone and there are ways that you can be grateful for events that have happened in your life so far which we will discuss later.

Worrying about your future just fills your head with negativity and you will find it difficult to express gratitude in this situation. It is much easier to find things to be grateful for if you live in the moment. So just focus on the here and now and take a look around you. Who do you have in your life? What things do you have in your life?

So take a few minutes out each day to just sit quietly and live in the moment. Focus on the here and now and if something interrupts your focus then refocus to the moment. If you need to go to a "special place" to really live in the moment that's fine. Find somewhere that inspires you and visit this place daily to find things in your life to be grateful for.

At first glance this probably appears negative to you but please read on and you will understand what we mean by this. Everybody has had bad experiences in the past. Maybe you had a time in your life when you had very little money, or suffered an emotional break up or something that really made you feel bad.

What you need to do is think about how far you have come since those bad events occurred. If there was a time where you had no money, or very little, then be grateful that you have money now to provide for your family and buy the things that you want.

If you had a bad break up experience then express gratitude for the partner that you have in your life right now. Your experiences are going to be unique so the examples here might not apply to you. This doesn't matter as long as you understand the principle we are trying to get across here.

Don't do what most people do which is to dwell in the past and fill their head with negativity because of their previous mistakes. Use it as a positive exercise to compare where you were then to where you are now and be grateful for this change. Be grateful to yourself for having the strength and intelligence to make the transition as well.

When you first start out on your gratitude journey it is essential that you find the motivation every day to express your gratitude. It's easy to get caught up in life and forget to practice your gratitude. Don't do this because you will lose your momentum. We recommend that you set up a reminder system around your home / office for your gratitude.

At home you can put up visual reminders in the form of print outs or written messages. Place these in locations where you know you will see them regularly such as on your refrigerator, in your bathroom, next to your computer or TV and so on.

Most people have a smartphone these days and you can use this to set up audible alarms to remind you to think about and express your gratitude. It is easy with modern phones to setup a number of alarms every day so learn how to do this and set those alarms!

Use a calendar to schedule a section of each day where you will practice your gratitude. If you want to do this on your computer or mobile device then this is OK because you should be able to set up an alarm that tells you it is time for gratitude.

There are many benefits to living a life based on gratitude. Here are some of those benefits:

You will be aware of the abundance that already exists in your life
It will help you to have more abundance in your life
It will help you to minimize the stress in your life
It will make you a lot more optimistic about your future
It will provide you with an increased sense of community
It will improve your resilience to handling difficult events
It will increase your sense of emotional well being
It will increase the amount of physical activity in your life
It will help you to sleep better
It will improve your physical health
It will reduce feelings of depression
It will reduce feelings of anxiety
It will give your immune and cardiovascular systems a boost

Do some research online and find more benefits of gratitude. Create a list of the benefits which really resonate with you and are things that you really want. You can either write these down in your gratitude journal (excellent idea!) or you can create a computer document and then print the list out.

The purpose of this list is to provide you with the motivation to persist with your gratitude so keep the list near to your bed and read it when you get up in the morning. For added power read the list before you go to sleep at night. This will send the right signals to your subconscious mind and in time it will help you to achieve your gratitude goals.

The Internet is truly something that we all need to be grateful for. It provides us with a whole host of resources that we can use to derive inspiration to continue with our gratitude lifestyle. If you visit a website like YouTube.com you will find thousands of inspirational videos that you can watch to help you to keep going with expressing your gratitude.

There are many websites that host podcasts as well such as SoundCloud.com. These are audio files that people create for all kinds of reasons. Finding an inspirational podcast that you can listen to on the way to work is far better than listening to the normal dross that is served up by radio stations.

The good thing about podcasts in MP3 format is that you can listen to them wherever you go and whatever you are doing. You can play MP3 files on your phone so just add the audio files that inspire you and then play them whenever you need inspiration.

There are plenty of inspiring blogs that you can read as well. All of this is free and just demands a little of your time. Watching a 3 minute inspirational video can work wonders for you. Choose videos that help you to see all of the good in the world. That way you will find plenty of things that you can be grateful for.

Using words to express your gratitude to someone else is great and they will appreciate you doing this. But you can take this to the next level by writing down your gratitude for others. Did you ever receive a love letter from a girl or a boy when you were younger? If so how did this make you feel? It made you feel great didn't it?

Some people hold on to love letters and other written forms of gratitude all of their lives. The reason is that the written words mean so much to them and they can read them any time they want to feel really special. Why do you think that the greeting card market is so huge? The written word will always be powerful so take advantage of this.

You can start by writing short "thank you" notes to people. Think about why you are grateful to that person. What specifically did they do to help you? Be sure to include this in your thank you note.

With practice you can start to write longer letters to people that have really influenced your life and who you are very grateful to. It doesn't matter if you have not had contact with these people for a number of years. Don't send these letters through the mail. Deliver them personally and read the letter out to the person.

The reaction that you will get will make you feel amazing. Most people will be blown away that you appreciate them so much that you took the trouble to write them a letter expressing your gratitude. And not only that you delivered it to them in person. Obviously if the person lives far away then use the mail but be sure to provide ways that they can contact you.

Receiving an email or a phone call from the person receiving the letter is nearly as good as being there in person. Ask them if you can have a Skype call (or whatever messenger service you use). Be sure to enable video on this call to see each other. That way you can see for yourself how much your letter meant to them.

We all have to deal with problems in our lives. Most of these are small problems that we can easily overcome but sometimes we are faced with bigger problems that demand we summon our inner strengths to resolve. A lot of people will react very negatively to these problems and even to some of the smaller ones that they encounter.

So how do you react to problems that come up in your life? Do the bigger ones send you into a negative thought spiral and overwhelm you? When you live a gratitude based life you can see the good in all of the problems that crop up in your life.

The best way to do this is to see all problems as opportunities. They are a chance for you to grow as a person. Think about some of the bigger problems that you have faced so far in your life and how you overcame them. What did you do to resolve them? Who did you ask for help? How did you feel once the problem was resolved?

Make growing as a person something that you are really grateful for. In that way when the problems occur you can be grateful that you have the opportunity to learn and grow. Without growth our lives would be very dull. The opportunity to move out of your comfort zone by learning something new and solving the problem should be grasped by both hands.

After a while of practicing this it will become second nature to you to see all problems as opportunities. Problems in life are not unique to you – everyone has different problems that they need to resolve. So think about how you will grow by solving each problem and be grateful for this.

The easiest place to start with this is your family. Explain to them the benefits of a gratitude life and make a copy of your gratitude benefits list for them. Once they are convinced that it is the right thing to do then use ways to get them to participate in gratitude on a regular basis.

Why not get a whiteboard for your home that you can place in a convenient location for everyone and ask them to write on the board what they are grateful for? You can write all of these things down so that you always have space on the board for more entries. If one of your family members has not made an entry then persuade them to do this.

Each week you can have a gratitude review session over dinner. Read out the things that everyone was grateful for over the past week. Show your gratitude to everyone for participating and moving the family forward.

You can do this with friends as well. For people that are willing you can create gratitude buddies and inspire each other to express gratitude every day. Use social media if some of your friends live far away. You could setup a gratitude group on Facebook that each person can use to record their gratitude experiences.

It is likely that you will be pleasantly surprised how many people that you don't know on Facebook request to join your group. Welcome them all with open arms and tell them what they need to do. If they are new to the subject then tell them to look at some of the previous posts to get an idea what they need to do.

There are just so many good reasons why you should live a life of gratitude. You will become an optimist rather than a pessimist, you will attract more good things in your life and there are physical and mental health benefits as well.

We have provided you with 12 easy and powerful ways that you can use to think about what to be grateful for and express your gratitude. All of them are easy to understand and apply so start using them right now and transform your life with gratitude.

Activity:

Gratitude Journal

Every evening, spend a few minutes writing down some good things about your day. This isn't limited to major events. You might be grateful for simple things, such as a good meal, talking to a friend, or overcoming an obstacle.

Give Thanks

Keep your eyes open throughout the day for reasons to say "thank you." Make a conscious effort to notice when people do good things, whether for you or others. Tell the person you recognize their good deed, and give a sincere "thank you."

Mindfulness Walk

Go for a walk and make a special effort to appreciate your surroundings. You can do this by focusing on each of your senses, one at a time. Spend a minute just listening, a minute looking at your surroundings, and so on. Try to notice the sights, sounds, smells, and sensations you would usually miss, such as a cool breeze on your skin, or the clouds in the sky.

Gratitude Letter

Think about someone who you appreciate. This could be a person who has had a major impact on your life, or someone who you would like to thank. Write a letter that describes why you appreciate them, including specific examples and details. It's up to you if you'd like to share the letter or not.

Grateful Contemplation

Remove yourself from distractions such as phones or TV and spend 5-10 minutes mentally reviewing the good things from your day. The key to this technique is consistency. Think of it like brushing your teeth or exercise—it should be a normal part of daily self-care. This technique can be practiced as part of prayer, meditation, or on its own.

Gratitude Conversation

With another person, take turns listing 3 things you were grateful for throughout the day. Spend a moment discussing and contemplating each point, rather than hurrying through the list. Make this part of your routine by practicing before a meal, before bed, or at another regular time

Overlooked blessings:

What overlooked blessings do you have to be grateful for right now?

_____
_____
_____
_____
_____
_____
_____
_____
_____
_____
_____
_____

Positive things about my health & body:
What things are you grateful for about yourself?

_____
_____
_____
_____
_____
_____
_____
_____
_____

Activities I enjoy:
What helps you enjoy the moment without thinking of anything else?

Relationships I am grateful for:
Who are you grateful for in your life?

PART 7
Ways To Achieve a Positive Mindset

CHAPTER TWENTY SEVEN
Ways To Achieve a Positive Mindset

People with positive mindsets are wonderful to be around with. They're a force to be reckoned with. They are so full of life that you'll often feel like you have no choice but to feel great about yourself, too. Even if life throws them under the bus, they're going to climb back up and go about their positive ways. They're resilient and optimistic, that's what they are.

If you're feeling sorry for yourself right now because you're not exactly a positive thinker, don't worry. In this short report, you're going to find out seven ways you can achieve a positive mindset. Note I didn't mention the word 'easy.' That's because transitioning over from a negative mindset to a positive one will take a lot of work. Are you ready? Let's get started then!

Remove Negative Words From Your Vocabulary

This point sounds pretty easy, doesn't it? You're probably thinking all you have to do is just figure out which words are negative, and then refrain from ever using those again! Well, the harsh truth is it's easier said than done.

Our thoughts can pretty much come out of nowhere. If you've been a negative thinker for far too long, then you'll be hearing those negative words in your mind whether you like it or not. So, this is where self-awareness and self-control come in.

With self-awareness, you'll know precisely when you're about to launch into a negativity-laced tirade whether it be against yourself or someone else. You'll know it because you can feel the negativity building inside you. If you're self- aware, you'll put a stop to it. Douse the fire with water, so to speak. That way, you're not going to be hurting yourself nor will you hurt other people with your verbal attack.

So, what do you do then? Well, you can either silence your negative inner voice or you can swap out those negative thoughts with positive ones. Your choice. Depending on the scenario, you may want to just keep your mouth shut if you think you can't find the right (positive) words to say. Then when you've cleared your head and thought things through, then say those positive words. You'll feel better, and the person or people you're speaking with won't be affected by negativity.

All of us should understand how words work. They're powerful, that's for sure. So, make it a habit to say positive words with a more positive attitude.

CHAPTER TWENTY EIGHT
Tell Yourself You Can Do Whatever You Put Your Mind To

In order to make this happen, you need to do something first
– you need to believe in yourself. Otherwise, no matter how many times you tell yourself you can do it, but if deep inside you're doubting yourself, then nothing's going to happen.

You can work hard all you want, but you won't get very far. Without self-belief, you'll essentially be blocking your own path to success.

Self-belief is one of the core characteristics of a positive person. By default, if you strongly believe in yourself and what you can do, then you've got healthy self-esteem. You feel good about yourself. You hold yourself in high regard.

Believing in yourself is such a simple but powerful thing to do. You can quite literally achieve anything that you set your mind to. There are no limits out there, only those that you impose upon yourself.

Determine the things that you truly want and set how you want to live your life. Then take action to achieve those plans. It's never too late to start creating the life of your

dreams. Dream realistically, start small and don't ever give up.

Remember, no one will achieve your dreams for you but yourself. You have to go after what you want, or else you will be boxed into the kind of life you'll end up hating later on.

Personal Story:

In October of 2010 I was 28 years old. Had an ten year old autistic daughter. Was working my up the managerial ladder. By December I was on the verge of divorce going back and forth between trying to work things out and something wasn't right.

Starting in January or 2011 I would start my year of hell. In and out of the hospital with unknown reasons to being ill. Dropping weight too fast to be healthy. At the same time trying to hide the stress so my daughter wouldn't see how bad mommy was.

Then it happen. June of 2011. They found the cause by a hail Mary test. One helicopter flight to the nearest neuro hospital and I was told I needed emergency surgery before a thing in my brain ruptured. So at 28 I was making out my will and getting my affairs in order for my daughter's long term care.

Now surgery was put off for a few weeks during which time I had my first stroke. I went from always active to now being partly immobile.

Sounds horrible right?

Now lets fast forward two weeks. Brain surgery and having another stroke while under the knife. Waking up half blind, speaking a language no one knew, and being partly paralyzed.

The Doctor looking at me and saying I would **NEVER** walk again without a walker maybe a came. **Never** speak normal again.

Never...

There was so many negatives there I shut down. I spent the next two weeks in the woe is me, kind of depression.

But here's the thing I had the wonderful daughter that needed me. I can't live the rest of my life in a hospital bed.

So I found my why.
Now I have to tell myself I have to get better. Then I will get better.

Ok I can't do: and fill in the blank I had a list of what I thought I couldn't do. But I also made a list of what I could do.

I can write with use of computer. I can read.I can learn new languages. I can do PT .

Now I could say how hard that first year was with pain. I could go into the depression and all of the negative. But by telling myself that I can and forcing my mindset to grow I am able to speak English which you can hear on my radio show. I can walk pretty normally most of the time.

Now I will say I have limits of what I can do. However, everyday I push those limits despite pain. I pay for it later. Yet I do it so that my today is a little better than my yesterday.

My point is simply this If I can over come 2011 then you can overcome just abut anything that you put your mind to. It is up to you to control what is your truth and change what you put your mind to.

If you would like to go in detail about my year of hell please reach out as I am open to discuss the mindset to over come this.

CHAPTER TWENTY NINE
Stop Dwelling On The What- Ifs And Focus On The Present

Daydreaming about the past is not going to do you any good. The simple fact is you're going to be missing out on your present because you got too caught up imagining the what-ifs of your past!

What good is it going to do for you now if you made a different choice in the past? Nothing, right? You'll only be making yourself even more miserable. Instead, what you can do is learn from your past so you can live fully in the present.

Focusing on the "now" isn't so easy either. There are far too many distractions all around us which tries to pull our

attention in many different directions. To help you focus on the "now," you can start practicing on being mindful.

With mindfulness, you literally experience what's going on around you right now. It helps increase your awareness, it helps you become more alert of what's happening in your surroundings. Focusing on the present moment allows you to appreciate what you currently have in your life. Instead of looking somewhere else, you can hone in on what you should be grateful for.

Living in the present with one foot stuck in the past is simply not a good idea. You'll never find true happiness, and you'll never feel fulfilled. The best thing to do is to make peace with the past and let bygones be bygones.

CHAPTER THIRTY
Surround Yourself With Positive People

Not everyone around you is a positive person. You may be surprised to hear this, especially if you don't just let random people into your life. It doesn't matter if they're family or friends, some people are the polar opposites of positivity.

If you've got friends who don't accept you for what you are, or they spew negativity into your ear all the time, or they

don't value you at all, then perhaps you'd like to distance yourself from those people.

The good news is that there are many positive people in this world, so you're not exactly limiting yourself if you stay away from your negative friends. Quite the opposite, in fact. You'll be freeing up space in your life to let positive people in.

The good thing about having positive friends is they actually encourage and motivate you to let even more positive people in. Whereas when you have negative people for friends, they suck the air out of you. Instead of expanding your horizons, they force you to narrow it down.

Having positive relationships with the right people will allow you to develop a level of positivity in your life that you've never experienced before! Letting go of negative friends and replacing them with positive people are two of the best things you can do to help you achieve a positive mindset.

Activity:

Associating with Winners

Did you know your income is the average income of the people you spend most of your time with? Want to double your income? Start hanging around people who make twice what you're making. You'll start thinking big, acting big, and earning big.

Seriously.

Successful people will tell you that you become like the people you surround yourself with. So surround yourself with Successful People.

Take a moment to describe a person that you think is successful and be very specific about why you think they are successful. Use these questions to help guide you in your answer:

1) What qualities do I most admire in these people?

_____
_____
_____
_____
_____
_____
_____

2) What qualities have I gained or desire to gain from these people?

_____
_____
_____
_____

3) Who are the 3 most influential people in my life?

Are You Happy

CHAPTER THIRTY ONE
Always Look At The Bright Side When Things Go Wrong

I cannot express this enough, but life is so much more worth living when you have a positive outlook and positive disposition. When you look at the bright side of things, you'll feel better mentally and emotionally, because you don't let any negative thoughts come in and linger in your heart and mind.

When you're optimistic and positive, you will naturally see all the good that life has to offer. When everyone else around you can only see darkness, you will see the light. You know there's always a silver lining somewhere, and you're not going to lose sight of that fact.

Another thing I'd like to point out is that when you come across as a positive person, you'll attract even more positivity in your life. You'll meet more positive people with the same set of healthy and positive habits and values as you.

You know how your actions impact others? Well, other people's actions also impact you. So, if you hang out with a positive group of people, then you're going to be influencing and making a positive impact on each other's lives!

Even when things go wrong around you, if people see you continuing to enjoy life, then you'll inspire them to do the same. Encourage those around you to live their life to the fullest and with no regrets.

You have every reason to be happy. You continue to be blessed with life, some people didn't have that luxury today. Life is too short. One day, you won't have the benefit of a new day so don't take life for granted.

Have A Bit Of Humor When You Encounter Negative Things

Humor goes a long way. It's an excellent coping mechanism that can help relieve your anxiety and stress. Think about all those times you've laughed out loud at something funny on the television or YouTube. You felt really good after laughing, didn't you? It's like a weight has been lifted on your shoulders and you can finally move around freely.

When you're able to see the funny side of things, you get the sense that everything is going to be alright. It makes you more resilient to all the challenges that life throws at you which in turn makes you a more optimistic person.

When you smile and laugh, you're essentially blanketing all your pain and your fears and smothering it with positivity.
Sure, they're not totally going to go away, but at least the pain and the fear is going to be put at the back of your mind. It's not going to be the first thing that comes to your mind.

When you have a sense of humor, you can pretty much handle anything.

Did you know having a sense of humor helps you lower your risk of cardiovascular diseases? Or that it lessens or delays the effects of aging? Sounds amazing, right? That's because it really does! And best of all, having a sense of humor won't cost you a dime!

When you learn to laugh genuinely, you will literally take years off your face. The truth is that happy people not only look healthy, but they look younger too!

Fail Forward And Learn From Your Mistakes

For those afraid of failing, let me ask you this question. Why are you afraid? What are you afraid of? Is it because you don't want to lose face in front of other people? Are you afraid of being labeled a failure by your peers or your family?

Whatever the reason, you're going to have to learn to put it all behind. If you want to achieve a positive mindset, you will need to learn how to embrace failure. The path to achieving positivity is riddled with hardships and challenges. If you fall

down and you let it put you off or scare you from following your dreams, then you're not going anywhere.

Successful people have had their fair share of failures. In fact, they have probably failed more times than the average person. But they didn't let that stop them from chasing their dreams. Instead, they've learned the art of failing forward.

Failing forward is not rocket science. It's all about accepting you've failed, moving on, and learning from your mistakes. When you use failure as a stepping stone towards success, then there's literally nothing that can stop you.

Failure is an inevitable part of life. Sooner or later, you're going to have to face failure, and you should be ready for that. Have a Plan B, C, D, or even more, in case Plan A fails. When you're equipped with a positive mindset, you can defeat failure in its own game.

Are You Happy

For those afraid of failing, let me ask you this question...
Why are you afraid? Are you afraid of? Is it because you don't want to lose face in front of other people? Are you afraid of being labeled a failure by your peers or your family?

Whatever the reason, you're going to have to learn to put it all behind. If you want to achieve a positive mindset, you will need to learn how to embrace failure. The path to achieving positivity is riddled with hardships and challenges, if you let them

down and you just fight your way through, you'll find yourself far from where you want to be... without anything.

Successful people have had their fair share of failure in fact, they have probably failed more times than the average person. But they don't let that stop them from chasing their dreams, instead, they've learned the art of failing forward.

If falling down is inevitable, it's alright...
or getting you feet in a running grip, and recoiling from your mistakes. When you use failures as a stepping stone towards success, then there's literally nothing that can stop you.

Failure is an inevitable part of life. So rather than you're going to have to face failure, and you should be ready for that. Have a Plan B, C, D, or even more. In case Plan A fails. When you're equipped with a positive mindset, you can determine its path on its own terms.

CHAPTER THIRTY TWO
Other Thoughts

Transitioning from a negative mindset to a positive one is hard, but very doable. Many people before you have succeeded and turned their lives around, so there's no reason why you shouldn't succeed, too!

A positive paradigm shift will bring long-lasting happiness and fulfillment into your life. You'll no longer be weighed down by negative thoughts and emotions. Your future will look so much brighter when all the dark clouds are gone. Embrace positivity and share it with the people around you!

Be aware of your inner thoughts are they the negative

"I feel like I'm up against the world."

"I'm no good."

"Why can't I ever succeed?"

"No one understands me."

"I've let people down."

"I don't think I can go on."

"I wish I were a better person."

"I'm so weak."

"My life's not going the way I want it to."

"I'm so disappointed in myself."

"Nothing feels good anymore."

"I can't stand this anymore."

"I can't get started."

"What's wrong with me?"

"I wish I were somewhere else."

"I'm worthless."

"I can't get things

"I hate myself."

together."

"Wish I could just disappear."

"What's the matter with me?"

"I'm a loser."

"My life is a mess."

"I'm a failure."

"I'll never make it."

"I feel so helpless."

"Something has to change."

"There must be something wrong with me."

"My future is bleak."

"It's just not worth it."

"I can't finish anything."

If so take a deep breath and choose to replace the thought with one of these:

"I'm proud of myself."

"I feel fine."

"No matter what happens, I know I'll make it."

"I can accomplish anything."

"I feel good."

"I'm warm and comfortable."

"I feel confident I can do anything I set my mind to."

"I feel very happy."

"This is super!"

"I'm luckier than most people."

"There are many people who care about me."

"I'm fun to be with."

"I will finish what I start."

"I will be successful."

"I am comfortable with life."

"I am respected by my peers."

"I take good care of myself."

"There's nothing to worry about."

"I am a lucky person."

"I have many useful qualities."

"There is no problem that is hopeless."

"I won't give up."

"I state my opinions with confidence."

"My life keeps getting better."

"Today I've accomplished a lot."

"I am in a great mood."

"I'm proud of my accomplishments."

"My future looks bright."

"I have a good sense of humor."

"I deserve the best in life."

"Bad days are rare."

"I'm happy with the way I look."

"I'm so relaxed."

"My life is running smoothly."

"Life is exciting."

"I enjoy a challenge."

"My social life is terrific."

"I have friends who support me."

"I have a good way with others."

"I have many good qualities."

Are You Happy

"My future looks bright."

"I am comfortable with life."   "I have a good sense of humor."

I am respected by my peers.   "I deserve the best in life."

"I take good care of myself."   "Birthdays are nice."

"There's nothing to worry about."   "I'm happy with the way I look."

"I am a lucky person."   "I'm so relaxed."

"I have many useful qualities."   "My life is running smoothly."

"There is no problem that is hopeless." "Life is exciting."

"I won't give up."   "I love a challenge."

"I share my opinion with confidence." "My social life is terrific."

"My life keeps getting better."   "I have friends who support me."

"Today I've accomplished a lot."   "I have a good way with others."

"I am in a great mood."   "I have many good qualities."

"I'm proud of my accomplishments."

PART 8
The Proper Mindset For Health & Fitness

CHAPTER THIRTY THREE
Getting Started

It happens so very often – we resolve to go on with a health and fitness program with gusto and probably much fanfare too, but in the first week of entering the program, everything fizzles out.

Why is it that we don't stick to the diet plans, the morning jogging plans, the workout plans that we make?

And what can we do to ensure we keep on with these plans, for our own sake and for the sake of the people that are dependent on us?

There are 5 basic reasons that I will list here bust we will go over in the next chapter along with how to stick with our plan.

1. YOU USE EXERCISE TO PUNISH YOURSELF OR COMPENSATE FOR YOUR DIET

2. YOU THINK EXERCISE IS "ALL OR NOTHING"

3. YOU DO TOO MUCH, TOO SOON

4. YOU DON'T EAT ENOUGH

5. YOU HATE YOUR EXERCISE ROUTINE

It's very important to do get healthy however you have to do it for the right reasons. With that said lets dive into how we can achieve a healthy mindset for health and fitness.

Are You Happy

CHAPTER THIRTY-THREE
Getting Started

It happens as very often – we resolve to go out with a healthy and fitness program with gusto and probably much fanfare too, but in the first week of entering the program, everything fizzles out.

Why is it that we don't stick to this diet plans, the morning jogging plans, the workout plans that we make?

And what can we do to ensure we keep on with these plans, to our own sake and for the sake of the people that are dependent on us?

There are 5 basic reasons that I will jot here but we will go over in the next chapter along with how to stick with our plans.

1. YOU USE EXERCISE TO PUNISH YOURSELF, OR COMPENSATE FOR YOUR DIET.

2. YOU THINK EXERCISE IS 'ALL OR NOTHING'

3. YOU DO TOO MUCH TOO SOON.

4. YOU DON'T EAT ENOUGH

5. YOU HATE YOUR EXERCISE ROUTINE

It's very important to do get healthy, however, you have to do it for the right reasons. With that said, lets dive into how we can achieve a healthy mindset for health and fitness.

CHAPTER THIRTY FOUR
Why Do Most Health and Fitness Programs Fail?

In today's world, rarely do any health and fitness programs work.
What's the reason for their alarming rate of failure?

Why Do Most Health and Fitness Programs Fail?

We hear it a lot – Someone takes a gym membership and then lets it die without a whimper. Someone takes up a diet and then returns to gluttony the next weekend. Someone does a great deal of expensive shopping from big-name brands for morning routines and then wears the filthily expensive tracksuit for lounging around at home. This bug is all around us – People make grandiose plans to start health and fitness programs and then let go of them at the drop of a hat. What goes wrong?

When we hear about the failure of diets or gym programs all around us, usually it isn't their fault. Usually it is the fault of the people who started with much hoo-ha about going through these programs, telling all their friends and colleagues about it, and then did not follow those programs through to the end. The people who leave midway do not see the benefits, of course, and the commercial fitness enterprises lose their face.

What the world needs today isn't a new health or fitness program, but it needs motivation. It needs the right kind of mindset to follow through with whatever program they have chosen to the very end. If they can do that, most of the health problems that are related to lifestyle situations will become passé. And we don't have to travel to the corners of the earth to find this motivation. The motivation lies right here, within us; we only need to search it and use it.

And this we need to do before even thinking of joining a health program.

So the next time you see that a program has failed or is receiving a lot of criticism, remember that the criticism isn't probably because the program stands on shaky ground. In most cases, it is because people began with great intentions and then did not follow the program as they should have.

Personal story:

2019 I was going thru a rough divorce and decided to do all of things I had been wanting to do but told myself that I couldn't. And then dragged my mom along with me.

One of those things was get a gym membership. Yes you read that right. The woman who had two stokes and brain surgery went and got a gym membership.

Add to that I had my mom also join.

For me , I was going to regain some more of my mobility. Adding strength training and core training. I want to be in the best shape I can be. It helps to have a place to go that is 100% my time.

Now my mom is a different story. She was going because I was dragging her out of the house. It wasn't her goal, or her way to do things. Now did it help her in the short term? **Absolutely**! However, for long term she with the help of 2020 decided not to stick with it.

My mom was doing something not because her mindset was wanting this but because I, her daughter , wanted her to do it. If she had wanted it for herself the she may have stuck with the workout routine.

CHAPTER THIRTY FIVE
Determination and Motivation – Your Most Important Allies

The main thing you need is motivation. As it is true in everything in life that you do, it is true here as well.

Determination and Motivation – Your Most Important Allies

The most important thing that you need to keep your health and fitness program alive – even more important than an instructor or a doctor – is your own motivation. You have to be determined to take stock of the situation. So, you are overweight and are looking at shedding some pounds. No gym instructor from anywhere in the world will help you if you don't take adequate measures to have the right diet and to stick with your routine exercise. Even if you are sick and are looking at treatment, no doctor will help if you aren't determined in following the treatment program, whether it is taking the medication at the right time or abstaining from some foods.

Why, even God doesn't help people who don't help themselves.

So, before even thinking of going ahead with a fitness or a health program, the one thing you need to be sure of is your own determination for it.

You have to make sure you will be motivated to carry on the program till the end. The best way to do it, of course, is to think about the end result. If you are planning to enter into a weight loss program, you could think about the great body you will have if you follow the program for a few weeks. In fact, you could go right ahead and shop for some jeans or even a bikini which is five sizes smaller than you are presently. The people who sell you that will think you are nuts, but you know what you are trying to achieve. Actually, stand up and tell them that this is what size you will be when you enter their shop again!

The same applies for every health and fitness program. If you have some cardiac ailment right now, think about how sticking to the right medical program will make you after a few weeks. You will be able to do things as before; your life will be richer.

The best way to keep yourself motivated is always to think about what is to come. Think about the result of your efforts. The efforts you need to put in won't seem so very difficult then.

Activity:

Finding Your Weight Loss Why:

What is my weight loss goal?
_____
_____

Why is this my goal?
_____
_____
_____
_____

Why do I want to achieve this goal?
_____
_____
_____
_____
_____

WHY is this important?

How does this make you feel?

WHY are you so determined now?

Finding Your Fitness Loss Why:

What is my fitness goal?

Why is this my goal?

Are You Happy

Why do I want to achieve this goal?

WHY is this important?

How does this make you feel?

WHY are you so determined now?

CHAPTER THIRTY SIX
Selecting the Right Program

It is highly important to choose the right program from the crowd.

Selecting the Right Program

The health and fitness industry is probably the most saturated industry in the world today. Part of the reason for that is people try out one program and then fail because of their own lack of determination and then think the program is worthless and try another. What the health and fitness industry doesn't tell people on their face is that they are failing mostly because they are not able to resolve themselves to stick to one program. They will probably fail with this one too because their minds are rolling stones, but it doesn't matter because presently they are spending thousands of dollars on buying their products.

It works that way. But the fact is that the industry is saturated. So what do you do when you are looking at a program for yourself? If it is a health treatment program, your choice is simpler. You just go to a doctor that you have faith in – usually your family physician – and then do as they say. But the issue is very much complicated if you are looking for a viable fitness program. What do you use to stay fit – diet, exercise, aerobics, calisthenics, what?

Researching on the Internet is not the answer. What you will find mostly is articles full of sales pitch, written by people who are trying to promote their own product. They won't have any qualms in painting some other perfectly good product with a negative color if they can improve the impression of their own product. The world gobbles it, so it works.

Now, if you want to choose a program, the best thing you could do is to head to your nearest bookstore. You should first narrow your

choices to two or three fitness programs that really interest you. It is great if you get to speak to some people who have used the programs you are contemplating on and who have absolutely no commercial interests whatsoever in promoting what they are doing. Join a health and fitness club. This is a great place to meet people who are conscious about their fitness and they won't mind giving you great advice. Many fitness clubs have their own libraries too, so you could find a lot of educational material in them.

When you get the books on what you are thinking about, take time out and read them. Read them mainly to understand what you will have to do, how much time you will have to devote, what equipment you will need, whether you will be able to do what is mentioned, what the results will be and how soon you will get them, etc. These facts will help you decide whether you want to be with the program.

Don't trust anybody when it comes to deciding a fitness program for you. Most people will have commercial interests. Some well-meaning souls will give you advice too, but they may be limited in their knowledge. It is best to speak with impartial experts, like your doctor, or read books and form an initial decision. Of course, you need to speak with a qualified person before making your eventual decision about what program to take.

Here's what my program looks like after introducing Consistency:

Day	General Activity
Sunday	Rest
Monday	Workout
Tuesday	Workout
Wednesday	Workout
Thursday	Workout
Friday	Rest
Saturday	Rest

As you design your fitness program, keep these points in mind:

Consider your fitness goals.
Create a balanced routine.
Start low and progress slowly.
Build activity into your daily routine.
Plan to include different activities.
Try high-interval intensity training.
Allow time for recovery.
Put it on paper.

Are You Happy

Here's what my program looks like after introducing Consistency:

Day	General Activity
Sunday	Rest
Monday	Workout
Tuesday	Workout
Wednesday	Workout
Thursday	Workout
Friday	Rest
Saturday	Rest

As you design your fitness program, keep these pointers in mind:

- Consider your fitness goals.
- Create a balanced routine.
- Start low and progress slow.
- Build activity into your daily routine.
- Plan to include diverse structures.
- Try High Intensity Interval Training.
- Allow time for recovery.
- Put it on paper.

CHAPTER THIRTY SEVEN
Starting Slow

Fools rush in; wise men take things one at a time.

Starting Slow

The key is to start slow. When you start your health and fitness program at a slow pace, you are much more comfortable with it and you get used to it better.

So, when you are embarking on your fitness regimen, don't commit the mistake of taking long strides right from the start. This is especially important when you are going to do things your own way. For example, if you are going to go jogging each morning, don't plan on jogging for an hour right from the first day. Start slow – maybe do just 10 to 15 minutes the first day. You probably haven't exercised since a long time. Hence, there might be a problem with your stamina too. When your stamina increases, you will be able to exert yourself for longer. But if you think of going the whole hog right from the start, you will be exhausted to the point of giving up.

The same applies when you are trying to go on a diet. You could not possibly give up all your favorite foods all at once. This will actually put you into depression and make you give up promptly. Depression also does something that will be detrimental to your weight loss plan. It releases a hormone known as cortisol. This hormone – also known as the stress hormone – will make you mentally weak and will make you vulnerable. You will give up your plan sooner because of the release of this hormone.

Instead, you could start by giving up a few of the unhealthy foods at the start and work them out of your schedule slowly – probably over a week or something. Even when you are on a strict diet, it is advisable

to have at least one interesting meal per week so that you don't feel too stressed out. In fact, you will be looking forward to that special meal each week.

When someone is trying to give up smoking, this is the approach followed. They are told to go on a reduction system, where they begin cutting down on the number of cigarettes they smoke each day. Over time, they drastically reduce their extent of smoking.

Thus, when you are trying to get into a long-term health and fitness plan, it is not right to start drastically all at once. Start slow and then build up the momentum. That's the way it will work for the long term.

1. Assess your fitness level

To assess your aerobic and muscular fitness, flexibility, and body composition, consider recording:

Your pulse rate before and immediately after walking 1 mile (1.6 kilometers)
How long it takes to walk 1 mile, or how long it takes to run 1.5 miles (2.41 kilometers)
How many standard or modified pushups you can do at a time
How far you can reach forward while seated on the floor with your legs in front of you
Your waist circumference, just above your hipbones
Your body mass index

2. Design your fitness program

Consider your fitness goals. Are you starting a fitness program to help lose weight? Or do you have another motivation, such as preparing for a marathon? Having clear goals can help you gauge your progress and stay motivated.

Create a balanced routine. Get at least 150 minutes of moderate aerobic activity or 75 minutes of vigorous aerobic activity a week, or a combination of moderate and vigorous activity. The guidelines suggest that you spread out this exercise during the course of a week. To provide even greater health benefit and to assist with weight loss or maintaining weight loss, at least 300 minutes a week is recommended.

Start low and progress slowly. If you're just beginning to exercise, start cautiously and progress slowly. If you have an injury or a medical condition, consult your doctor or an exercise therapist for help designing a fitness program that gradually improves your range of motion, strength and endurance.

Build activity into your daily routine. Finding time to exercise can be a challenge. To make it easier, schedule time to exercise as you would any other appointment. Plan to watch your favorite show while walking on the treadmill, read while riding a stationary bike, or take a break to go on a walk at work.

Plan to include different activities. Different activities (cross-training) can keep exercise boredom at bay. Cross-training using low-impact forms of activity, such as biking or water exercise, also reduces your chances of injuring or overusing one specific muscle or joint. Plan to alternate among activities that emphasize different parts of your body, such as walking, swimming and strength training.

Try high-interval intensity training. In high-interval intensity training, you perform short bursts of high-intensity activity separated by recovery periods of low-intensity activity.

Allow time for recovery. Many people start exercising with frenzied zeal — working out too long or too intensely — and give up when their muscles and joints become sore or injured. Plan time between sessions for your body to rest and recover.

Put it on paper. A written plan may encourage you to stay on track.

3. Assemble your equipment

You'll probably start with athletic shoes. Be sure to pick shoes designed for the activity you have in mind. For example, running shoes are lighter in weight than cross-training shoes, which are more supportive.

If you're planning to invest in exercise equipment, choose something that's practical, enjoyable and easy to use. You may want to try out certain types of equipment at a fitness center before investing in your own equipment.

You might consider using fitness apps for smart devices or other activity tracking devices, such as ones that can track your distance, track calories burned or monitor your heart rate.

4. Get started

Now you're ready for action. As you begin your fitness program, keep these tips in mind:

Start slowly and build up gradually. Give yourself plenty of time to warm up and cool down with easy walking or gentle stretching. Then speed up to a pace you can continue for five to 10 minutes without getting overly tired. As your stamina improves, gradually increase the amount of time you exercise. Work your way up to 30 to 60 minutes of exercise most days of the week.

Break things up if you have to. You don't have to do all your exercise at one time, so you can weave in activity throughout your day. Shorter but more-frequent sessions have aerobic benefits, too. Exercising in short sessions a few times a day may fit into your schedule better than a single 30-minute session. Any amount of activity is better than none at all.

Be creative. Maybe your workout routine includes various activities, such as walking, bicycling or rowing. But don't stop there. Take a weekend hike with your family or spend an evening ballroom dancing. Find activities you enjoy to add to your fitness routine.

Listen to your body. If you feel pain, shortness of breath, dizziness or nausea, take a break. You may be pushing yourself too hard.

Be flexible. If you're not feeling good, give yourself permission to take a day or two off.

5. Monitor your progress
Retake your personal fitness assessment six weeks after you start your program and then again every few months. You may notice that you need to increase the amount of time you exercise in order to continue improving. Or you may be pleasantly surprised to find that you're exercising just the right amount to meet your fitness goals.

If you lose motivation, set new goals or try a new activity. Exercising with a friend or taking a class at a fitness center may help, too.

Starting an exercise program is an important decision. But it doesn't have to be an overwhelming one. By planning carefully and pacing yourself, you can establish a healthy habit that lasts a lifetime.

Are You Happy

be strenuous. Maybe your workout routine includes various activities such as walking, bicycling or rowing. But don't stop there. Take a weekend hike with your family, go swimming, or try ballroom dancing. Find activities you enjoy to add to your fitness routine.

Listen to your body. If you feel pain, shortness of breath, dizziness or nausea, take a break. You may be pushing yourself too hard.

Be flexible. If your routine isn't quite right, give yourself permission to take a day or two off.

5. Monitor your progress.

Retake your personal fitness assessment six weeks after you start your program and then again every few months. You may notice that you need to increase the amount of time you exercise in order to keep improving. Or you may be pleasantly surprised to find that you're exactly where you want to be to meet your fitness goals.

If you feel motivated, set new goals or just allow yourself exercising with a thought of building a healthier fitness better may help, too.

Starting an exercise program is an important decision, but it doesn't have to be an overwhelming one. By planning carefully and pacing yourself, you can establish a healthy habit that lasts a lifetime.

CHAPTER THIRTY EIGHT
Target the Right Parts of the Body

Specialization and prioritization are two essentials if you want to do things the most efficient way, especially when it comes to deciding a suitable health and fitness plan for your needs.

Target the Right Parts of the Body

One of the biggest problems in following health and fitness programs arise when people don't know what they should really do. This makes them try out things that they shouldn't be doing, which actually prove ineffective for them. Not just that, but they also spend time and exert themselves in doing worthless things.

Take the example of someone who needs to gain muscle on his chest. Now, if this person tries a workout routine that focuses on other parts such as his legs, he wouldn't be doing a very wise thing. There are many exercises that can target the chest specifically. Finding out about them and using them in your methods can bring the quickest results.

That is what you need to do. When you are looking at a health and fitness program for your needs, look for a specialized one that will provide you the benefits you are looking for. This ensures that you get your results quickly and because you don't overexert your entire body, you have better chances of keeping up with the program.

In fact, some people try prioritizing their fitness regimens. They see what they need to do first and focus their energies on that. When that aspect of their fitness has improved, they move on to another. Such focused attention works quite well, especially in today's world when we are cramped for time and don't want to spare the effort either.

That is why most of the gyms have a structured program for working out. If you are joining a gym after a long time of physical inactivity, you will find that they will instruct you to focus more on building your

stamina first. For that, you might be asked to work on the treadmill or an exercise bike a lot initially. Once you have built up your system's capabilities, they will ask you to slowly start with resistance training. But, before that you might work out with a lot other things. You might be focusing on one particular aspect one fortnight and then move on to another area. This actually helps you – you are working out as per what your body needs.

Now, if you were to go all out at once, you would end up stressing your body to the max and this could be disastrous to your long-term planning. You might stretch your body so extensively that you will not be able to lift a finger. When that happens, people don't stick to their fitness plans.

The mistake here isn't of the program itself; it is of the way in which you approached it.

CHAPTER THIRTY NINE
Get Your Friends Involved

Friends can help in a lot of ways when you are trying to keep up with a health and fitness program. They could be the support system you need and could motivate you immensely.

Get Your Friends Involved

Your friends could be quite instrumental in making you stick with your fitness plan. Many health and fitness advocators say that if you work out with a friend, you do much better. If you have someone to go to the gym with you, or diet with you, or accompany you on your morning jogs, you stick much better to your routine and to the program itself.

There are many reasons why it works. The main reason is that the boredom does not creep in when you have a friend to work out with. We aren't bored when we are with our friends, are we? Also, there might actually be a healthy competition triggered between the two of you. You might want to see who can lift better weights, who can jog more, who can diet better, etc. All this keeps you highly involved in your fitness program and also quite motivated.

In fact, if you have a friend to accompany you in your health and fitness programs, you will actually start looking forward to that time of the day when you can work out with them.

But even if you cannot get someone to work out with you, you could involve them in other constructive ways. Just tell a few good friends that you are starting a health program. They will be all for it. They will even give you suggestions on the best ways to do it. But, suppose that all of that doesn't happen. They don't give you suggestions and, on the contrary, they start mocking you. Even that will help. You can take their mockery in the right spirit. When friends tease you, you get the fire burning inside you that tells you to show it to them. Consciously or

otherwise, you will double up your efforts just to show them that you can do it. Your friends keep you motivated even when they don't know they are doing that.

The next time you feel like gorging on that pastry when you are with a friend who knows you have started a diet, you will think twice. Chances are you will pass the pastry on. You won't eat it. That is because you won't like to falsify your resolve in front of a friend. But if you haven't told your friend about your fitness program, you would have no qualms about bringing with them.

This is how friends help you. Even if they don't say anything, and are actually unlikely to do so, they create a feeling in you that makes you want to stay with your health and fitness program.

CHAPTER FORTY
Chart Your Progress

Keep aware of how you are changing for the better. It encourages you to keep changing for the better.

Chart Your Progress

A very important thing for you to do when you are on a fitness program is to keep checking how you are progressing. This can keep you highly motivated, especially when you see that you are becoming what you want yourself to become.

So, when you are on a diet program, weigh yourself often, doesn't matter even if you do it several times a day. When you are jogging, check how many steps you can climb without breathing. When you are working out at the gym, keep checking your abs and chest. When you are on a program to improve your blood sugar level or your blood pressure, keep monitoring yourself. In fact, go for more frequent physical checkups just to see how well you are progressing.

Humans are very much result-oriented people. We want to see facts and figures – we want to see things as raw as they can be. This is the reason why charting your progress continuously can help you immensely.

When you see that your waist size has come down from 38" to 36", when you see that you can get into skimpier shorts, when you see that you are closer to touching your toes than before, you become very much pleased with yourself. You see that your efforts are bearing fruit. This keeps the fire burning.

Initially, you will want to monitor yourself quite often. Your family may even mock you for that. But it doesn't matter. You need to know where you are heading. So keep looking as much as you want. It is

only when you are in love with your body that you will think of doing something for it. And no one loves your body more than you, so the onus of making it fitter and healthier is entirely on you.

You have every right to know how your body is shaping up. The best part is that this eggs you on to do better for your body. So keep monitoring yourself and keep working out to your heart's content.

CHAPTER FORTY ONE
Keep the Motivation On – Give Yourself Incentives

Rewarding yourself is one of the best ways to ensure that you keep doing the right things.

Keep the Motivation On – Give Yourself Incentives

Time and again, reward yourself for your achievements. However, don't reward yourself with a food treat; that will only make matters worse. In any case, we are too much fixated on food. When we are happy, the first thing that comes to our mind is a treat that involves the worst kinds of unhealthy foods possible. And this is what brings on most of the health problems that we face today. We could do much better from a health point of view if we cured our fixation with food.

But you could always give yourself a healthy incentive. You could go on a trip, for example. You could take a break from work and simply hang out at home, watching DVDs. Or you could cook a healthy meal all by yourself at home if that interests you.

However, the best incentive is looking in the mirror. When you see the improved shape you are in, you will want to congratulate yourself. In fact, you should keep some of your old photos for comparison. When you know how well you have turned out so far, you will want to go all the way. You will feel that it is quite possible for you to take further steps.

Go shopping. Buy clothes that fit your newly reworked body. You will be so happy about buying jeans that are two sizes smaller. You will feel you have achieved something special.

Are You Happy

You have to understand something here – When you measure yourself at home and see that you have reduced, you are happy. But you become much happier when you reward yourself for it. When you buy smaller waist jeans you see the practical connotations of your fitness program. You actually see the benefits. This is what motivates you to keep working on in the future. If you see these benefits and then begin rewarding yourself for it, you will see that you are able to push you toward better health and fitness achievements.

CHAPTER FORTY TWO
Head to the Gym... Even if You Don't Want to

Get yourself to the gym each day, even if you don't think you want to work out. Just heading out to the gym can help you immensely.

Head to the Gym... Even if You Don't Want to

One of the ways in which you can motivate to keep working out is by simply taking the effort to go to the gym. Research shows that most people who quit their gyms don't do it because the exercises are too stressful to them; they do it just because they don't want to make the trip to the gym! Sounds corny, but it is true. If you have joined a gym before, you will be aware of this feeling. You don't mind the exercises, but you do feel bored about putting on your gym gear and heading out to the gym, which is probably too early in the morning for you.

If you don't want to go to the gym on one particular day, try this ruse. Try telling yourself that you will just warm up a bit on the treadmill and then move out. Tell yourself that you won't do anything that needs you to exert much. When you convince yourself that way, you are likelier to head to the gym.

But when you are there, you will see a change happening in your way of thinking. When you see all those people diligently working out there, you will get motivated too. And when you start out on the treadmill, you will find that your stamina is building. When that happens, you will tell yourself that you could try one more exercise. You might go on to the exercise bike. That may induce you to go to the weights and then the resistance training and so on. Sooner than you think, you will find that you have had your complete workout!

Studies show that this approach works in 90% of the cases. i.e. 90% of the people who come to the gym reluctantly, thinking that they will only work out for 5 minutes, end up working out their full routine.

The same applies with other things. If you are feeling lazy about going for jogging, convince yourself by saying that it is only for a few minutes. You might tell yourself that you would do nothing more than one lap around the park. But when you are into it, you feel that you might as well complete the whole thing.

CHAPTER FORTY THREE
Ensuring You Stick to Your Health and Fitness Program

You can keep going, just be convinced that you can.

Ensuring You Stick to Your Health and Fitness Program

Given the large rate of failure of health and fitness program worldwide, it is easy to see why anyone will have a fair share of apprehension when they try to get into such a program themselves. They are bound to think whether such programs will work for them or not. Even when you join a gym, however much enthusiastic you are, somewhere in the corner of your mind you wonder how long you will be attending the gym. Such damaging feelings start when you haven't even had your first workout at the gym.

Mainly this happens because the world over people are joining health and fitness programs and then leaving them midway, reducing even very well-meaning programs to mockery. It is their weakness that makes them quit, but the world doesn't waste any time in jumping to the conclusion that something is not quite right with the program.

One of the best favors you could bestow upon yourself is to condition your mind into thinking positively about the program you are about to join. Don't keep any space for pessimism. There is no reason why you should think that the program won't work for you. Think that it will work. Think about all the benefits you will get because of that. Think about your sexier body shape, your healthier heart, your improved physical capacity, and you will want to carry through.

Think about how you will become a better individual. Think about how you will be able to travel to all those places when you are healthier.

Think about how your bank balance will improve because you will become more productive. Think about how you will get better prospects at work because you are healthier. An improving professional life is what sets most of us thinking.

Also think about how you will be able to spend more quality time with your friends and family. Think how you won't be the one sitting in the corner when they are having fun right in front of you. You will be able to join in the revelry as well. If nothing works, take a look at your children, if you have them. Wouldn't you like to be with them for a longer time? Wouldn't you like to see how they progress in life under your guidance?

We come back to square one actually. The best thing to make any health and fitness program work is the right motivation. And determination. You have to make sure you keep yourself pepped up so that you follow through till the end. See yourself in a newer light. That will really help this highly important task you are embarking upon.

CHAPTER FORTY FOUR
Final Thoughts

There it is – Everything you need to to start building a happier you. From mindset to fitness. But please keep in mind this is only a start. It will be a long process to start seeing results and keeping them.

It all starts with you. Soon you will be seeing a new you. A Happier You, but only if you put in the work.

Just because your perspectives have changed. Just because you know now how you must start with your health and fitness programs so that you follow them through for life. The journey for a happier healthier life starts today but must continue everyday.

I wish you all the best in your journey. For additional exercises , journal activities and yummy recipes please pick up Are You Happy   Everyday Happiness: A Guide to Finding You

For one-on-one coaching connect with me at www.MLRuscsak.com

Are You Happy

About the Author

Melisa is all about authenticity, as anyone who's met her can attest. Whether you've seen her speak or talked with her at an event, or had a conversation with Melisa she is relaxed and candid. In the same way, her speaker bio doesn't just share the standard info about her credentials and speaking skills

"Motivational Keynote Speaker, Melisa Ruscsak works with individuals and organizations to amplify their communication, connection, and confidence so they can make an influential impact on the world. She mentors with passion, guiding her clients to effectively strengthen and elevate their leadership vision to new heights.

With over five years of corporate training experience, a knack for making meaningful connections with audiences, and an insatiable appetite for helping others maximize their potential, Melisa knows how to rock a platform, connect with a crowd and provide training so that others can effectively do the same.

Melisa's down-to-earth humor compels audiences to laugh while they learn. She engages groups from the moment she steps in front of them and leaves them with empowering tools and focused mindsets that they will use long after the lights have gone out on the event. Melisa is passionate about people, leadership, and successful businesses. She is especially inspired to help people take their careers - and themselves - to unprecedented levels.

When not speaking or training, Melisa can be found creating new worlds and stories within her literary world. Those works can either be found in stories for young adults or housed within screenplays.